THE KING, CRUCIFIED AND RISEN

The King, Crucified and Risen

Meditations on the Passion and Glory of Christ

Fr. Benedict J. Groeschel, C.F.R.

CHARIS

SERVANT PUBLICATIONS
ANN ARBOR, MICHIGAN

Charis Books is an imprint of Servant Publications especially designed to serve Roman Catholics.

Servant Publications—Mission Statement

We are dedicated to publishing books that spread the gospel of Jesus Christ, help Christians to live in accordance with that gospel, promote renewal in the church, and bear witness to Christian unity.

Scripture verses are taken from the Revised Standard Version of the Bible, copyright 1946, 1952, 1971 by the Division of Christian Education of the National Council of Churches of Christ in the USA. Used by permission.

Published by Servant Publications
P.O. Box 8617
Ann Arbor, Michigan 48107
www.servantpub.com

Cover design: Alan Furst, Inc., Minneapolis, Minn.

02 03 04 05 06 10 9 8 7 6 5 4 3 2 1

Printed in the United States of America
ISBN 1-56955-289-4

Library of Congress Cataloging-in-Publication Data

Groeschel, Benedict J.
  The King, crucified and risen : meditations on the passion and glory of Christ : daily readings from Ash Wednesday to divine mercy Sunday / Benedict J. Groeschel.
    p. cm.
  ISBN 1-56955-289-4 (alk. paper)
  1. Jesus Christ--Passion--Meditations. 2. Jesus Christ--Resurrection--Meditations. 3. Lent--Meditations. 4. Devotional calendars. I. Title.
  BT431 .G76 2002
  242'.34f--dc21

                                                            2002011589

Contents

A Word of Thanks

It would be impossible for me to keep up with all the publishing and writing I have to do without the assistance of several people. I am particularly grateful to my friend and associate Charles Pendergast, who has provided a great deal of the effort in preparing this manuscript. He was generously assisted by a priest who wishes to remain anonymous. I also want to thank Bert Ghezzi and all at Servant Publications who assist me in every way.

I also wish to express sincere gratitude to my own staff at home: our secretary, June Pulitano, and our receptionist, Karen Killilea, who make it possible for me to accomplish all that I do. I am also deeply grateful to our volunteers, particularly Cathy Hickey, Roberta Ronan, and Carol Vunic, without whose assistance I would have no time at all.

I expect to share this volume with many who have assisted our Franciscan community and our work with the poor, especially in the foreign missions, and I hope that the book will be a spiritual blessing for them.

Fr. Benedict J. Groeschel, C.F.R.
Solemnity of Pentecost, 2002

Introduction

You and the Need for Personal Prayer

Many good people ask me, What can I do personally to come closer to God, to Christ? Then almost despondently they ask, What can be done to restore morality, faith, human dignity, family values, respect for life, and Christian hope and charity to our de-Christianized world? Even though religion and faith still occupy an important place in our society, they are obviously losing ground. Devout members of the Church wonder what can be done to restore Christian education, renew the clergy and religious life, and inspire the laity.

A serious reading of Church history—a story of growth and decline and growth again, of fervor followed by apathy and, surprisingly, by reform and renewal—gives us a resounding answer to all these questions. The solution lies in personal prayer, a real, substantial commitment of individuals to prayer.

Throughout history there are innumerable examples of those dedicated to Christ through prayer in every major Christian denomination of East and West. We think of early Church reforms led by people like St. Augustine and St. John Chrysostom, the monastic reforms of Sts. Basil and Benedict, and the monastic revivals in the

East by Sts. Sergius and Tikhon. We recall the fervent preachers of Catholic reform in the West—Sts. Bernard, Francis, Dominic, Catherine of Siena, and Ignatius—as well as the Protestant evangelists Johann Arndt, John Wesley, Jonathan Edwards, and Phoebe Palmer, to mention only a few. They called people to a life of reform through prayer.

St. Catherine of Genoa, a remarkable woman reformer and mother of the poor in the troubled time on the eve of the Reformation, summed it up by teaching that all reform must begin in the individual heart. And how does one enter into the heart except by prayer?

A single example will illustrate the point very well. In the turbulent sixteenth century a woman who described herself as a worldly nun began a reform that still produces remarkable contemplative saints. How did she do it? She tells us very simply, "I began to practice prayer." And St. Teresa of Avila did this very seriously, meticulously, and with a sprightly personality that we do not generally associate with contemplatives.

Her method of prayer is so simple that it will serve as a guide for these meditations on the suffering, passion, death, and Resurrection of our Lord Jesus Christ. I intend these meditations for all Christians, for anyone who believes that Jesus Christ is the Incarnate Son of God, who for our salvation suffered, died, and rose again and who lives forever. If you want to grow as His disciple, these meditations may be helpful for you.

What This Book Is About

In the first of this series of meditations on Christ, published as *Behold, He Comes*, we considered the mystery of Christ's eternal origin, His human conception and birth, and the beginning of His life among us. Although these meditations were organized in such a way that they could be used from the First Sunday of Advent to the Feast of the Epiphany, they were not keyed specifically to the Catholic liturgy of the day; thus other Christians might easily use them. Obviously I derived much inspiration from the liturgy of the Advent and Christmas seasons, but I wanted to include Christians who are not Catholic and who do not have a liturgical tradition. Also I wanted to make these meditations useful at other times of the year for anyone wanting to have a deeper appreciation of Jesus Christ and the mysteries that surround Him. I am doing the same thing in this book so that it can be used by anyone seeking to grow in the prayerful appreciation of Christ's life of struggle, suffering, and death, His way to the Cross, and His glorious Resurrection.

How to Pray With This Book

In other books I have suggested a simple form of meditation drawn from the experience of St. Teresa of Avila. This method is so simple that its usefulness may be overlooked. If you learn this method, it will remain with you as a very helpful piece of spiritual equipment.

1. Calm your body and your thoughts. Reflect on the fact that you are going to listen to the voice of God. For these meditations it is best to have your Bible at hand.

2. In silence call on the Holy Spirit to help you pray and pray well. St. Paul teaches us that the Holy Spirit prays within us (Rom 8:26–27). Remember that prayer is the lifting up of the mind and heart to God. The mind refers to our thoughts, and the heart to all our desires and feelings, even the inmost ones of which we are not ordinarily aware.

3. First read the brief Scripture passage thoughtfully at the beginning of the daily meditation. Then read the meditation, taking your time. Go back over things you want to ponder more deeply or that you do not completely comprehend.

4. Let the thoughts sink into your mind. Ask yourself, What do these thoughts about Christ lead me to? How do I respond to them with my heart?

5. Sum up your prayer, first by meditating on the short prayer following the meditation. This is only to help you make up your own prayer, using your own thoughts and words. Make your prayer time as long as possible. Speak to Christ, and firmly believe that He blesses your prayer mysteriously and knows you better than you know yourself. He says constantly to us, "Come to me, all who labor and are heavily burdened, and I will refresh your soul.... For my yoke is easy, and my burden light" (Mt 11:28, 30).

6. Finish your prayer with some resolution or decision to follow Christ more closely this day. He calls all who follow Him to change. He Himself provides what is necessary for us to change,

but we must accept this grace. "Come to me, all who labor and are heavily burdened, and I will refresh your soul.... For my yoke is easy, and my burden light."

Although the burden of the Christian life is ultimately much easier than a life without meaning or one without a promise of life beyond this world, nevertheless Christ describes discipleship as carrying the Cross. "If any man would come after me, let him deny himself and take up his cross daily and follow me" (Lk 9:23). These meditations are written with the hope that those who read them will change and that they will carry their cross. Pray that I who write them will change as well.

A Word About Lent

Most of us are unaware that times of penance, fasting, and prayer for forgiveness are part of the traditions of many of the world's great religions. Most Christians are aware that our Jewish neighbors observe Yom Kippur, or the Day of Atonement, as a time of fasting, penance, and asking for God's mercy and forgiveness. Most of us do not know that Jews have other similar observances during the year.

As many Muslims make their homes among us, we now are becoming familiar with Ramadan, a whole month of complete penitential fasting, even from water, from sunrise to sunset. The early Christians were familiar with a similar period observed by the Roman pagans in February, a name that means the month of whips, so called for the scourges they used for self-discipline and penance. In fact, that is why the ancient Romans made this cold, dark month the shortest of the year.

In early Christian times the custom of fasting and penance was adopted by the Church in East and West to prepare for the solemn commemoration of the passion, death, and Resurrection of Christ, which were celebrated during the Sacred Triduum, or the three holy days at the end of Holy Week. The oldest Catholic custom outside the prescriptions of the New Testament—the making of the sign of the Cross—was linked with the traditional biblical sign of penance, the imposition of ashes on one's head. The ceremonies of Holy Week, beginning with Palm Sunday—the commemoration of Christ's triumphant entry into Jerusalem—brought the time of Lenten penance to a dramatic close with the observance of the Easter Vigil.[1] The origin of all these customs, paralleling the Jewish observance of Passover, was a powerful need both to acknowledge gratefully Christ's gift of Himself for our salvation and to instruct people on the meaning of the events in salvation history.

Unfortunately, the observance of Lent has become modified to such an extent that many do not really observe its penitential spirit. They are consequently deprived of experiencing the profound spiritual renewal of the Sacred Triduum and the recommitment to their baptismal promises made to Christ at Easter.

Even the word *Easter* is somewhat unfortunate, coming, as it does, from the pre-Christian Germanic observance of spring. In Latin and its derivative languages, the name is the Feast of the Resurrection. In the East, people still joyously greet one another at Easter with the

---

[1] See James Monti, *The Week of Salvation: History and Traditions of Holy Week* (Huntington, Ind.: Our Sunday Visitor, 1993).

words "Christ is risen" and the reply "He is truly risen."

Many early Protestant denominations did not observe any of the Christian holy days, dismissing them as superstitious observances. For instance, it is rather well known that New England Protestants did not observe Christmas (the date is not given in the New Testament but was chosen by the early Church to take the place of the Roman festival celebrating the "birthday of the sun," or the winter solstice). What seems to be more puzzling is that they did not observe even Holy Week or Easter. These observances were kept by Anglicans, Episcopalians, Lutherans, reformed Protestants, people in the Methodist tradition, as well as the Catholic and Orthodox immigrants. Eventually Calvinist and Baptist churches began to observe these days selectively.

Catholic and Orthodox Christians often observe their liturgical celebrations at slightly different times, but this does not represent a different tradition. Actually, it hearkens back to an acceptance or a rejection of the calendar reform by Pope Gregory XIII in the sixteenth century. Now the vast majority of those who call themselves Christians appear to observe these days in some ways, but this is diluted by the secularism of our culture.

If You Are Reading for Lent

If you reading this book in Lent, let me encourage you to fast in any way you like. You may try simply to avoid eating between meals and to eat only one full meal a day, which is the traditional modern way to fast. People ordinarily do not fast on Sunday. You can always give up some special treats. In the Eastern and Slavonic traditions some people observe the black fast, which means also abstaining from meat and dairy products.

Many people make sure that during Lent they help the poor and perform works of charity and social justice. Many still spend additional time in prayer, and it is not uncommon to see large numbers of people at daily Mass or at evening services in Protestant churches. If you do some or all of these things, you will be surprised. At Easter you will want to shout joyfully, "Christ is risen." At least a bit of the joy of Mary and the disciples will be yours on the day of the Resurrection.

Lent

Ash Wednesday

"Yet even now," says the Lord, "return to me with all your heart, with fasting, with weeping, and with mourning; and rend your hearts and not your garments."

JOEL 2:12

Ashes are an external sign of penance and a reminder of God's certain judgment of our deeds. In the Jewish Scriptures those who were aware of God's judgment after they had fallen into sin, like King David, used ashes to indicate their penance.

It is interesting to note that in New York City, a very worldly but also a surprisingly religious city, a proportionately larger number of its citizens obtain ashes on Ash Wednesday than do the residents of any other city in America. Thousands of people who are not Catholics crowd the churches to receive ashes and be reminded that they are dust and unto dust they shall return. For many this perhaps expresses a desperate hope that their earthly trial will soon be over.

Whether one receives ashes or not, Christ's message in the Gospel is clear enough: Entrance into the kingdom of God requires repentance. There are several steps to real and effective repentance, as all members of twelve-step groups can tell you.

These twelve steps, as they are outlined by Alcoholics Anonymous, are in complete agreement with the Gospel. The Gospel teaching makes clear the fact that we must recognize our powerlessness to save ourselves and that we must rely on Christ for salvation, as well as for the grace to accept this salvation from Him. We need to be thoroughly honest with ourselves about our sins and especially about unchristian ways of thinking and unholy desires. We would be wise to confess our weakness honestly and completely to someone.

In the Catholic and Orthodox Churches this confession occurs in the sacrament of reconciliation, or penance. Personal confession to another person, especially to a minister, is becoming more common-place now in other churches, as it was at the time of the Reformation.

If the opportunity for confession is not available, then at least we should make a realistic appraisal of our failures to be a real follower of Christ. This is best done every evening in a quiet but honest review of what we have done during the day. Then we need to speak to Christ in the depths of our heart and express our deep regret at our failures, indifference, and lack of commitment to Him. The words "If you love me, keep my commandments" (Jn 14:15) can be a power-ful opportunity for us to examine our conscience and experience a sense of repentance.

Finally we must make amends by following Christ's counsels in the Gospels to do good and to heed His words. "Everyone will be rewarded according to his deeds" (see Mt 16:27). When practicing any virtue or performing any works of mercy, we also must acknow-ledge openly that we depend wholly on Christ's grace.

If you are reading this thoughtfully, you are probably saying to yourself, "I have a lot of catching up to do." This is exactly what can happen in the next forty days. What will you do with these days?

Prayer

Lord Jesus Christ, Your words in the Gospel are very direct. You called all around You to a fuller, more complete, and growing pursuit of the kingdom of God within. During these days of Lent help me to read Your words every day and follow them more faithfully. Let me be honest with myself and not deny that there is much for me to do in order to become Your real disciple. Then take me by the hand and draw me along so that I may follow You. Amen.

Thursday After Ash Wednesday

I have set before you life and death, blessing and curse; therefore choose life, that you and your descendants may live, loving the Lord your God, obeying his voice, and cleaving to him.

DEUTERONOMY 30:19-20

If you love me, you will keep my commandments.

JOHN 14:15

Lent is a time for choosing. For most people reading these pages, it is a time for renewing choices made many times before. That can be a problem. The recognition that we often take two steps forward and one step back can be discouraging in itself. We begin to question our own sincerity.

The fact is that we must repeat and renew our choices over and over again. This is especially the case when the behavior we want to get rid of or avoid, or the new approach we want to take, is at odds with our true deep feelings or when we have mixed motives. "I would like to choose the right, the love of God, life," many of us say, "but not if it's too demanding." Moses knew very well what he was saying when he told the Israelites: Choose life or choose death.

Even people who work hard at being good Christians will find areas in themselves that are still in need of conversion. St. Paul's advice, "Press on!" is very much aimed at this realization of our divided inclinations and desires. Conversion is a lifelong process.

Through God's providence I have heard the confessions of people who may be canonized as saints. They had no difficulty finding attitudes and actions in themselves that needed a more complete conversion. And I have at times heard the confessions of old sinners who could not remember anything to confess.

Often our conscious resolutions to change come to nothing because we don't know ourselves. We all have powerful dynamisms or energies operating in us—the need to live, or to love and be loved, or to be happy. We may have a disproportionate need for security or acceptance. We may hate and love ourselves at the same time. To begin, with the help of the Holy Spirit, to know ourselves better is to prepare the ground for deeper conversion.

Get to know yourself, and make this Lent a time of choosing, of going down inside and asking, Do I really choose life? Do I really keep the commandments as Christ indicated they must be kept by those who love Him?

Prayer

Lord Jesus, give me the light of Your Holy Spirit that I may more clearly choose the life You came to give. Help me to really repent on a truly deep level, and help me genuinely to lead others around me to a more Christian life and a more honest and complete discipleship. Amen.

Friday After Ash Wednesday

If a man fasts for his sins, and goes again and does the same things, who will listen to his prayer? And what has he gained by humbling himself?... To keep from wickedness is pleasing to the Lord, and to forsake unrighteousness is atonement.

SIRACH 34:26; 35:3

And Jesus said, "This kind of devil can only be cast out by prayer and fasting."

MARK 9:29

Have you ever walked into one of those incredible new supermarkets and asked yourself what your grandmother would have thought about all of this—or if you are still quite young, what your great grandmother might have thought? Most items are available in several brands and in varying styles and even with a selection of deadly details—from superlight to very rich, from no-cal to chocolate bomb. And when you check out, despite your bargain card, the total bill can be daunting. We are a rich and pampered society, often misled by advertisements for junk food. The expression itself is significant.

Lent is a great time to eat only what we need but not the best or the most tasty. When we get to know some of the saints through reading their lives, it becomes clear just how far most of us really are from fasting and self-denial. Fish on Friday can hardly be thought of as a penance when it includes lobster thermidor. Fasting means plain things—no frills, no fancy desserts—and experiencing a little hunger at least between meals.

Is there a difference between fasting and dieting? Yes. Dieting is a naturally good idea and can be motivated by reasons of health or vanity. Fasting is undertaken to remind us that we have no permanent place in this world and that we seek the world to come. It is a very real investment in eternity, or at least a reminder of the eternity we must seek.

If you happen to like good food (and if you don't, try some other penance, please), there is a tinge of the apocalyptic about fasting. Many other great cannoli or strudels may come along, but the one you deny yourself goes by forever. It will never come back. This denial reminds us that all pleasures will be gone one day.

Pleasure must never be the final goal of any action. Serving up a good meal or showing appreciation to the cook or saving some of our money to do good—all of this can be part of a motivated Christian life. Something as insignificant as a cookie can remind us that we all are pilgrims on our way.

Prayer

Lord Jesus, You have promised those who follow You that You will bring us to the heavenly banquet. Even after Your Resurrection You provided a mysterious breakfast for the apostles (Jn 21). You also fasted and prayed for us. Give me this little grace to fast, so that I may be Your true disciple and come someday to Your great marriage feast. Amen.

Saturday After Ash Wednesday

Jesus saw a tax collector named Levi sitting at the tax office; and he said to him, "Follow me." And leaving everything behind, he rose and followed him.

LUKE 5:27

Those who are well have no need of a physician, but those who are sick. I have not come to call the self-righteous, but sinners to repentance.

LUKE 5:31-32

As Lent goes on, you will look for ways to maintain your spirit of repentance. Keep in mind each day that you are trying to change, to improve your discipleship and friendship with Jesus.

You may say, "I don't commit deliberate sins." I hope not, because even a small deliberate sin is an awful thing when we recall that it is a deliberate action against the God who loves us. For most serious Christians it is not a matter of deliberate sins but of sins of weakness, committed when we are distracted or fatigued.

But these half-baked sins, if I may call them that, reveal a great deal about our underlying motives and attitudes. If they persist, they show what we think is really important, what resentments we still hold on to, how lackadaisical we can be in our love for God and our zeal for Christ. No human actions are completely random; everything we do has a cause, or rather a layer of different causes.

Coming to some realization of these attitudes and unconscious causes of our actions is what self-knowledge is all about. It is stupid to say, "Well, that's how I am. People will have to accept me for what I am." The only one who can say that with real conviction is God Himself. The rest of us have to look at ourselves and change.

To change in order to bring our lives into agreement with the Gospel teaching is a clear admission that we need God's help to follow Christ, not just by desire and words but also by deeds. As we begin Lent, let us try to acquire this mind-set. I am going to know myself and change. Why? Because He says, "Follow me." Back when the first disciples followed Him they heard Him say, "The time has come and the Kingdom of God is at hand. Repent and believe the good news" (Mk 1:15).

Prayer

Lord Jesus, to those who knew You, You were very forgiving but very challenging. You wanted those who knew You to think and act as much as possible according to Your example. "Follow Me," You said. Lord, give me the grace to see and know what I must really do every day in order to follow You. Amen.

Week One of Lent

The First Sunday

And Jesus, filled with the Holy Spirit, returned from the Jordan, and was led by the Spirit for forty days in the wilderness, tempted by the devil.

LUKE 4:1

Today is sometimes referred to as Temptation Sunday because the Gospel recounts Christ's temptation in the desert and because His fast of forty days parallels the fast of Lent. We also think of the temptations of the first human beings described in the third chapter of Genesis.

The first temptation led to an unimaginable catastrophe that has plagued our race ever since and will continue to do so until the end of the world. Your life and mine are constantly limited and frustrated by the effects of that original sin. Seldom do we recall that the difficulties of our lives are rooted in the confusion brought about by that original temptation and sin.

The temptation of Christ in the wilderness takes place at the beginning of His public life. It's as if He took on Satan, who had tortured the human race for so long, and defeated him in their very first encounter. This encounter, which we can only know from Jesus' own testimony—since there were no witnesses—follows the pattern of a rabbinic scriptural debate. This form may have been used by the evangelist when confronted with the task of describing an encounter between the Son of God and the Prince of Darkness, which no human being had ever seen.

St. Paul tells us that what is written in Scripture is for our instruction. The Church Fathers thought that the challenges given to Christ conveyed specific warnings to His followers. There is the rejection of self-indulgence, pride, presumption, and power. Later on Our Savior will refer to the prince of this world and his tools: the lust of the flesh or self-indulgence; the lust of the eyes, which can be seen as a desire for power over others like the kingdoms of this world; and the pride of life, pointed to by Satan's rather stupid suggestion that Christ do miraculous acrobatics.

Modern people don't think very often about Satan, or the Prince of Darkness. This is really surprising since the twentieth century saw several devastating wars and terrorism that can only be described as satanic. It is often only after the damage is done that people realize that they themselves have unwittingly played into the hands of evil. They did not know that they were shaking hands with the devil.

Perhaps if we were honest with ourselves, we would admit that even if we have never purposely done evil, we have gone along with it or kept silent when we should have protested against it. This is a very uncomfortable thought. Not even the apostles stood by their beloved Master when He went to His trial.

Any thoughtful person ought to be able to see the hand of God in the beauty of creation or in a generous and faithful soul. Christ is present on so many occasions that the believer often encounters Him without much thought or thanksgiving. But also unseen is the dark counterforce, the bleak and frozen opposite pole of evil. It may be monstrous like Auschwitz or the Gulag, or it may be unnoticed, like a young person driven by drugs or a politician selling out for the pro-abortion vote. It may be any one of us going along with the tide.

Lent calls each of us to resist temptation and to seek God's grace to do so. But it also summons us to see where we are involved with evil ourselves. Repent of the past briefly and quietly, and concentrate on the present. There is much for the Christian to do in our own immoral times. St. James sums it up very well: "To care for the widow and the orphan in their need and to keep oneself unspotted by the world" (Jas 1:27).

The apostles, including the great and zealous St. Paul, learned that they had to be vigilant all the time. Lent offers us an opportunity for silent self-examination, for looking inward in the presence of God, for listening to the inspiration of the Holy Spirit, for measuring our lives against the standard of the Gospel, especially the Sermon on the Mount.

A great help in doing this is the intelligent daily reading of the Bible, especially the Gospels. This is the living word of God, and it cuts deeply into the lies we tell ourselves. When Lent is over, we may feel a certain exhilaration when we realize that we have made progress toward the truth.

Prayer

Lord Jesus Christ, Your temptation teaches us so much. Give us the grace of the Holy Spirit to know what we must do and the strength to take the next good step. Strengthen us that we may recognize the works of darkness. Give us the grace to avoid participating in evil unknowingly. Give us the truth to know what is good, and do not let us be overcome by evil. Amen.

Monday

And the King will answer them, "Truly, I say to you, as you did it to one of the least of these my brethren, you did it to me."

MATTHEW 25:40

The prophets of Israel were very clear in their conviction that works of justice, generosity, almsgiving, and kindness were essential to penance:

Is not this the fast that I choose: to loose the bonds of wicked-ness, to undo the thongs of the yoke, to let the oppressed go free, and to break every yoke? Is it not to share your bread with the hungry, and bring the homeless poor into your house; when you see the naked, to cover him and not to hide yourself from your own flesh? Then you shall call, and the Lord will answer; you shall cry, and he will say, Here I am.

ISAIAH 58:6-7, 9

It is interesting to note that when people do works of charity, they require that the poor they help be destitute. Actually, in our country, very few people are destitute, but many live right on the margin of destitution, with little or no security and very few frills. Some will say, "Who needs frills?" We all need a few, and I mean need. I love to give presents to poor children and poor old people. They're not starving but few have ever given them something just because they are themselves. Is it really a frill for a child whose mother is on welfare to get a Christmas present, which she could not possibly afford to buy?

Do you want to have a great Lent? Tip the gas station attendant who doesn't speak much English. Tell the newsboy to keep the change, with a smile. Buy a cup of coffee and a doughnut for the fellow collecting aluminum cans to trade in.

Or go first-class. Send a poor child to Catholic school. Help an old lady on Social Security get her medication every month. Tell her you can get it at a discount, and just take a dollar to make her feel that she's paying for it. She's getting it at a discount from you.

Lent may be a time of penance, but if you are generous with the frills for God, then you will know that you have brought a smile to the face of Jesus Christ. Happy Lent.

Prayer

Lord Jesus, father of the poor, open my heart and look into my eyes and help me to be generous. Give me a generous heart so that I may really love You where You have said You may be truly found. Amen.

Tuesday

Your Father knows what you need before you ask him.

MATTHEW 6:8

Today the Church offers for our meditation the succinct and comprehensive summary of Christ's teaching about our relationship with the Father—the Lord's Prayer. In about fifty English words Our Lord, the Eternal Son, tells us what our attitudes must be toward His Father and our Father. Some have said, although it may be an exaggeration, that if we only had these words of Christ we could deduce everything else He taught. To begin with, this prayer glorifies God in His absolute divinity and transcendence—the quality that describes Him as being over and beyond all things. This act of adoration should be the beginning of all prayer so that we may acknowledge who we are before God and to whom we are speaking.

The first petition, "Thy kingdom come, Thy will be done," reminds us that God is all and that our only true happiness can be found in Him. This acceptance of God's will by free rational human beings is what is meant by the kingdom or rule of God in our lives and hearts. Although we have many needs and petitions, this one must overarch them all. This is why Our Savior said, "Seek first the Kingdom of God and His righteousness and all these things will be added unto you" (Mt 6:33). As we grow spiritually, we might estimate the degree of our spiritual growth by the purity and intensity of our desire for His kingdom to come.

Once the supremacy of God is clearly stated, we can ask for what we need. Christ says, "Ask and you shall receive" (Mt 7:7). He does not say we receive exactly what we request but that we will receive what is best for us.

Then comes the most demanding and mysterious of all Christ's counsels: to forgive as we are forgiven. "Love your enemies and do good to those who hate you and pray for those who persecute and calumniate you." It's the most mysterious command of all. But forgiveness is a necessary component of Christ's teaching. This is obvious from the important place He puts it in this prayer.

The familiar translation of the final petition, "Lead us not into temptation," is a bit confusing. A more accurate rendering, "Do not put us to the test but save us from the evil one," is clearer. It asks God's assurance and protection in the course of life, and even from the powers of darkness. How meaningful these words must have been to those who faced the innumerable evils recorded in history. Christ Himself would pray like this in Gethsemane.

This prayer is a gold mine of meditation and contemplation and should provide the background of every prayer we say. For this reason Our Lord introduces this prayer by telling us that this is the way we should pray.

Prayer

Heavenly Father, You are so mysterious, beyond anything we can imagine or conceive, but Your Son has given us this prayer to be said even by little children. Listen to the voice of Your beloved Son as we pray with Him for all we need. Amen.

Wednesday

This is an evil generation; it seeks a sign.

LUKE 11:29

The contemporaries of Jesus sought signs from Him that He was sent from God. In fact, He did perform many astounding signs and wonders, such as healing the sick and raising the dead. But they wanted a sign right in front of them at that very moment. When Jesus converted people, He always required an act of faith, a decision to believe. He said to Thomas, "Blessed are they who have not seen but have believed" (Jn 20:29).

It's interesting that literally thousands of people, apostles and disciples among them, had witnessed the wonders and signs that accompanied the preaching of Jesus. Yet except for the apostle John and the women who accompanied Jesus from Galilee, no one stood beside Him at the Cross. They needed more signs. If indeed He had come down from the Cross, as His enemies taunted Him to do, all of Jerusalem would have come singing hosannas. But there had to be a test of faith.

We live in a time when faith is tested. Many who once believed later openly disbelieve and leave the Church. Or they stay around to embody that pathetic reality that Jesus calls "little faith." They do not confess Him before men but rather stand at the edge of the crowd and let the ridicule of Christ go on. Sometimes they chip away at His message and find themselves straddling belief and secularism. And they consider this pathetic stance prudent. They might be better off if they tried a real secularism, a real worldliness without any grace at all. They would find how bleak it is. To put it poetically, they would taste the bitter grapes of wrath. Then they might take Christ Our Savior more seriously.

It is well to recall that Saul of Tarsus, Christ's bitter enemy, was called to conversion, and he listened and gave himself totally to the Savior whom he had persecuted. The rich young man, on the other hand, as far as we know, never came back to Christ. He probably spent the rest of his life dithering about it and telling people he had met Christ but was not quite sure of the validity of His message. Watch out for dithering Christianity. It's a good word to describe people who can't make up their minds. They never really say yes.

One sees a great deal of dithering in Christian circles right now:

Catholic colleges that are not even Christian, religious communities that are not religious, clergy and laity who are not committed witnesses to the saving message of Christ. We offer marriages and funerals, meetings and lectures. Where in the world is the burning flame that Christ came to cast upon the earth? "The men of Nineveh will arise at the judgment with this generation and condemn it" (Lk 11:32).

Prayer

Lord Jesus, shock me out of my complacency with Your grace. In every way that is open to me, let me be a real witness to You and the salvation You alone can give. Help me each day to confess You and not to be one who dithers back and forth. Amen.

Thursday

How much more will your Father who is in heaven give good things to those who ask him!

MATTHEW 7:11

When we pray, inevitably we find ourselves asking God for things. I used to feel guilty about this, but I gave up that particular guilt. It came to me that God obviously wants to give us things. God is a giver—the great giver. Consider God the Father in the incredible bounty of creation, God the Son in the immense riches of grace He obtained for us by His life and death, and God the Holy Spirit in His constant inspiration and His holding of all creation in existence from moment to moment. Giving, giving, giving. When we are trying to relate to such a Being, it is rather obvious that we should ask for things. This is precisely the advice Our Lord gives us: "Ask, and you shall receive; seek, and you shall find" (Mt 7:7).

The challenge is to ask in the right way; otherwise, religion becomes a grab bag, a kind of immature ritual. Those who go to God as spoiled children are entirely disappointed by Him. A thousand times I have heard the words, "I really prayed hard for ..., but God did not give it to me."

Christ promised that God would answer our prayers. "Ask, and you shall receive." He did not promise that we would receive exactly what we wanted or thought we needed. Rather, in answering our prayers, He gives us what is best for us in God's plan. How many times have you later realized that what you asked for would have been disastrous for you or someone else? God's will for us is the best.

What about obviously good things we ask for and do not receive? I think of the thousands of people who had loved ones in the World Trade Center and who prayed desperately but they did not come home. When people do evil things or nature gets unruly, as it does during an earthquake, many human beings can get caught in the way. They pray fervently, but apparently the worst happens anyway. Here is where faith must come in. After the shock, grief, and anger are past, one must sit down and decide to believe again in the goodness of

God. Often this is not as difficult as it may seem, because in the course of time we experience what St. Paul meant when he said, "We know that all things work for good for those who love God" (Rom 8:28).

But there are times when we cannot see any good. This is when we must believe and trust that God will bring the best out in eternity. If you have trouble doing this, think of the sorrows of the mother of Jesus. Surely she must have prayed that the cup of suffering would pass Him by. It did not. She held on until the Resurrection, only to lose Him again. She had to wait until the journey of her own life was finished. Yet it is clear from the life of the Blessed Virgin that although all things work together unto good for those who believe, it is never easy.

Prayer

Lord Jesus, increase my faith so that no matter what happens, I may believe and trust in You. Help me to know that I will receive the good gifts that I need to go on. Amen.

Friday

Unless your righteousness exceeds that of the scribes and Pharisees, you will never enter the kingdom of heaven.

MATTHEW 5:20

All our lives we have heard warnings about the scribes and Pharisees, and we have just assumed that we are not among them. Lent offers us a good opportunity to ask ourselves, Who are they, and who are we? The scribes, official copiers of the Bible in the days before printing and also conveyers of religious texts, were a class of professionally religious people. Religion was their business. Under the Romans they performed the important task of keeping the Law and the Jewish traditions alive. They were committed to seeing that there was no watering down in the direction of Roman paganism, which was all around them.

The Pharisees were strict and literal observers of the Law of Moses, and they constituted a religious-political movement that was profoundly hostile to Rome. Their opposite number was the Sadducees, who were much more influenced by paganism in their denial of the supernatural, even of life after death. All these groups grew hostile to Jesus, but only the Pharisees and the scribes saw themselves as seeking righteousness and the kingdom of God. The Sadducees were interested in getting along with the Romans and preserving Jewish culture. Because the Sadducees were in power, their high priest engineered Jesus' arrest and condemnation.

Readers of my books are probably not inclined toward modern-day Sadducism. My friends and I are on the other side. We need consistently to be on our guard against becoming Pharisees, straining out the gnat and swallowing the camel, to use the humorous example of our Lord Himself.

Right now Christianity is filled with conflicting opinions, disputes, and misunderstandings. This puts great pressure on bishops, pastors, religious superiors, and, in fact, on anyone running anything in the Church. If you try to walk honestly in the middle way, you may find yourself attacked from both sides.

The real danger is to be so upset by criticism that anger, insult, and even calling people fools become characteristic of our behavior. Christ warns us in Matthew 5:24-26 to be reconciled with others before we offer our gift at the altar. Our Lord warns us that we may end up "in prison" until we have paid the last penalty because of our anger. Many commentators have seen this as a reference to Purgatory, or the purifying journey after death.

The big question here is not who is right or wrong but who is angry. The Church faces such serious issues in our time as confused religious teaching, the failure of religious education, questions about liturgical and sacramental life, and the proper understanding of Christ's divinity. These are issues to get riled up about; they should not, however, lead us to the self-righteous anger of the scribes and Pharisees. The arrogant and self-righteous Pharisees did not allow themselves to hear the saving Gospel of the poor Messiah from Galilee. They could not believe even when they witnessed miracles as astonishing as the raising of Lazarus, a man dead four days. In a word, they were hard-hearted and judgmental. They despised Jesus because He taught with authority and reached out to the publicans and harlots, whom they considered the scum of the earth.

It is indeed essential to stand up for truth, even what we only suspect to be the truth, and not to flinch. At the same time it is important to avoid arrogance, self-righteousness, and rash judgment. Otherwise, Our Lord warns, we may be off to jail.

Prayer

Lord Jesus, You suffered much from the self-righteous—those who observed the Law but gathered to mock You at Calvary. Give us the Holy Spirit that we may see our own faults and try to be understanding. Grant that as sinners we may bear witness to Your truth and Gospel in such a way that we do not drive others away but rather bring them to You. Amen.

Saturday

I say to you, Love your enemies and pray for those who persecute you, so that you may be sons of your Father who is in heaven.

MATTHEW 5:44-45

The real test for gauging our progress in the spiritual life comes with the command to love our enemies. Anyone who has turned to Christ and is trying to follow Him needs to decide to follow this command, which is not just a piece of advice. But only those who have made some appreciable progress will be able to experience inwardly a degree of forgiveness and the peace that comes with it. The decision to forgive, if it is really sincere, is a beginning, but the real experience of inner forgiveness may take years of spiritual progress.

The reason is simple enough. The great and most difficult step on the Christian spiritual journey is to trust God, and to trust Him in whatever happens. Trust is the real turning point after moral conversion. Once that is achieved, the evil that men may do to us falls into a unique perspective. At worst they can kill the body, but they cannot kill the soul. Trust in God, properly understood, is the road to being able to forgive, although trust and forgiveness may not seem to be obviously related.

Because trust in God is a lifelong struggle, our Lord gives us several different motives (besides trust) for practicing forgiveness. The first is given in the Lord's Prayer: We have been forgiven by God ourselves. The second is expressed by Christ on the Cross when He prays for His murderers because "they know not what they do." The third and least obvious but the most powerful motive is that we will be like our heavenly Father, who makes the "sun rise on the evil and on the good" (Mt 5:45). We often misread the words, to be "perfect as your heavenly Father is perfect" (5:48), thinking that they call us to some godlike moral perfection. The context indicates that the perfection Christ refers to is the perfection of charity and forgiveness— that is, not leaving anyone out, the just or the unjust. Perfect in this context means universal or complete.

One of the goals of Lent is to take stock of oneself spiritually. This is not easy to do. Often we deny our faults or see ourselves in too positive a light; or perhaps we get pulled into a negativism, a kind of self-hatred that is paralyzing and hopeless. To some extent we are all like the persons AA members often describe themselves as being before they took the twelve steps—megalomaniacs with inferiority complexes.

A way out of this self-love–self-hate trap is to work toward forgiveness of others. A good first step is to analyze the motives, however disturbed, of those who may have hurt us. Second, we need to look at their personal histories: a dysfunctional family background, a limited education, a failure to achieve goals, a lack of spiritual development because of bad example or poor advice—all of these contribute to people's doing badly in life and hurting others.

Finally, we must ask ourselves what we would have done if we had been in their place. Would we have acted differently, or would we have done worse? While all of this is going on, we should remember that God, the Most Holy Trinity, wishes the salvation of every soul. Christ came and suffered for this purpose. If we want to be like our heavenly Father and His beloved Son, we cannot be filled with resentment and ill feeling. We must honestly and lovingly wish the salvation of all.

Prayer

Heavenly Father, give me the grace to know how much You love every human soul and how You desire all to be saved. You even sent Your Son to labor and to die for the salvation of each soul. May I not despise or wish evil on those whom You love. Rather let me be like You and extend myself even to my enemies. Amen.

Week Two of Lent

The Second Sunday

This is my beloved Son, with whom I am well pleased; listen to him.

MATTHEW 17:5

In the course of life we listen to many people. Some are wise, and some are foolish or at least misled. Some try to help us toward salvation, while others have no idea that life is a journey. It might be a helpful exercise to list in your mind all the people you listen to every day. These will include the recorded voice on someone's answering machine, the actor on television who tells you that you really need such-and-such an antacid, the news commentator who perhaps unknowingly distorts the truth, and the preacher who minimizes the divine message because he has not thought or prayed about it very much.

In the Gospel we are told by God Himself to listen to the Son of God. We move to an entirely different experience. In the Gospels there is no error, no possible perversion of His words to soften or alter His message. As His hearers long ago often observed, "He speaks with authority."

Why then do we not listen to Christ and put His words before all other words and ideas? Why don't we make every effort to follow them, even when it is difficult?—and it often is. Recall that we are told to seek first the kingdom of God, to enter by the narrow gate, to forgive and love our enemies and not turn away from them when they ask our help, to see and serve Him in the poor. We do not deny these counsels or commands, but we do not place them first among all the bits of advice, instruction, and information we receive. Newspapers, television, and the Internet may in fact occupy much more of our attention than the words of the beloved Son of God.

In days gone by, even not so long ago, the words of Christ were put over the doors of public buildings. In Budapest, great golden letters over the cathedral doors proclaim: "I am the way, the truth, and the life." Christ's words were treasured and written by hand in beautiful Bible manuscripts and later printed in beautiful books. Once in a while we see the Beatitudes or the Lord's Prayer on parchment, but rarely. His words, once solemnly sung in the liturgy, are now read. Often enough the sermon is in trivial contrast to the words of the beloved Son.

As Lent moves on, how helpful it would be to concentrate on some of the Lord's words. When I was in jail for saying the rosary outside an abortuary, I was allowed to keep only one book—the Bible. I used my time to read whole books of the Bible in one sitting, something I had never done before. Then I realized that there was something unique about the Gospels, something different even from the other inspired books. Each time I finished reading a Gospel at one sitting, I had the experience of knowing Jesus as I had never known Him before. In fact, the clarity of each evangelist's picture of Him, most of all the power of His words, electrified me.

Try to find the time to read an entire Gospel at one sitting—perhaps St. Mark's first, since it is the shortest. In Passiontide (the last two weeks of Lent) read the Gospel of St. John. When you are finished, a powerful word or idea will come welling up in your mind, quite independent of any decision or intention of your own. It will rise in your own thoughts: "This is Your Beloved Son in whom You are well pleased. I must listen to Him."

Prayer

Holy Spirit, give me the grace to hear the words of the Beloved Son at the center of my being and in the depths of my heart. Grant that in some way I may bring His words to those who know them less or not at all. Amen.

Monday

Judge not, and you will not be judged; condemn not, and you will not be condemned.

LUKE 6:37

As Lent progresses and our examination of conscience continues, we are guided by the words of Christ Himself and come, as we inevitably must, to the serious consideration of our own pride. Surely one of the best indications of inner pride is the need to judge others and even to condemn them. The issue is beclouded by our obvious responsibility to be morally discerning at the same time. In an attempt to avoid being judgmental, we cannot go through life blissfully accepting evil deeds or even foolish actions. The Christian must always separate the good from the bad and be able to recognize the fruits of each. In this case we must judge right and wrong. Not only did Christ do this, but He did it out loud. He said, "I did not come to judge the world, but to save the world" (Jn 4:7). How do we judge deeds without judging those who do them?

The question contains its own answer. We judge deeds and their consequences. We have no way of being sure of our own judgment of those who perform them. Progress in this endeavor is a long and very narrow way. On one side is moral responsibility; on the other side, self-righteous arrogance. The practical answer on how to follow such a narrow and straight way is to recall that we do not know how others were formed in their ability to make judgments. They may lack moral training or even intelligence.

Repeatedly I have seen well-intentioned people sell out or remain silent in the face of evil because of their own insecurity. Perhaps this is a family trait or even a result of much fear and anxiety in childhood. Perhaps it signifies a co-dependency, or a need for approval, acceptance, or success.

What becomes obvious is that many have no ability to stand up to evil. How few there were who went with Our Savior to Calvary, and in fact there is no record of any man speaking in His defense. A number of women did what they could, but they had no voice. The only person to lift a finger to help the Son of God was a pagan, the wife of Pilate.

This is a sad but revealing commentary on human nature. And this tragic insight leads to an inescapable conclusion: We all fail many times, and we would fail more often if we were put to the test. The answer to the question of judging bad behavior and those responsible for it is to be found in the advice of Jesus Himself. "Judge not,... condemn not." Why? Lest we be judged ourselves.

The Son of God came to save. He could warn people very directly, yet when He was betrayed, His words were an obvious appeal to the culprit to repent: "Judas, do you betray the Son of man with a kiss?" (Lk 22:48). We all need to meditate on judgment and righteousness. We must learn to distinguish between the sin and the sinner, the crime and the criminal.

The best way practically is to pray for the sinner and the criminal that they will see the error of their ways and change. If we just silently go along, we become partners in their sin. If we attack them, they will only become more defensive. If we tell it as it is, as clearly as we can without hurting them, and if we pray, then they may come around to the truth. Every case is different, and we must ask the Holy Spirit to guide us so that we will proceed justly and lovingly and seize the moment of truth when it comes.

Prayer

Jesus, help us by your inspiration to be honest and prudent, merciful and wise. Help us always to seek the salvation of others and to avoid the pride that makes us judge others when we should be judging ourselves. Amen.

Tuesday

For you have one master, the Christ.

MATTHEW 23:10

Lent is a time not only for penance but also for greater study and reflection on our Christian life. It is a time for us to get to know the teachings of Christ and to interiorize them or, as the early Christians would say, to write them on our hearts. Obviously the Christian has only one master, which means only one teacher. That person is Christ. This is what the Gospel means by the powerful Latin phrase: *Magister vester unus est, Christus.*

The best way to write the teachings of our Blessed Savior on our hearts is to study the Gospels and then the other books of the New Testament, which are the experiences and thoughts of those who either knew Jesus of Nazareth well or knew those who knew Him. One towering New Testament writer, St. Paul, knew Him only through a mystical and miraculous experience on the road to Damascus. But he came to know Peter and the other early disciples and became a very important part of the early Church.

There are two very important things to keep in mind when we read the Gospels and other New Testament books, and in fact when we read the whole Bible. The first is that there is no other writing like this book, because it is accepted by faith as the word of God. Christians have believed this from the time the various books were written over a period of several decades. They revered these writings as the divine word just as their Jewish forebears had with their Scriptures, which we refer to as the Old Testament.

The principal author of the whole Bible is the Holy Spirit, who by inspiration and providence guides the many different authors. This means that these writings are essentially without error. They cannot mislead, if properly understood, especially if understood as a whole.

A recent Vatican document suggests that the Bible is symphonic, like a great piece of music, which when taken as an integral whole is harmonious. Individual passages may appear to contrast with other ones. In fact, Our Lord uses just such contrasts in the Sermon on the Mount when He makes clear that His teaching goes beyond what came before Him. "You have heard that it was said, 'You shall love your neighbor and hate your enemy.' But I say to you, Love your enemies and pray for those who persecute you, so that you may be sons of your Father who is in heaven" (Mt 5:43-45).

The quality of inerrancy—that is, that the Scriptures, properly understood, do not deceive—does not mean, as fundamentalist Christians think, that the events described are historically precise in the way that modern news reports are perceived to be precise. (News reports seldom are.) One can see this by reading the four different Gospel accounts of Jesus' Resurrection. Each writer had his own point of view and sources of information. What they all agree on is that the Jesus whom the apostles knew really and physically rose gloriously from the dead and was seen by many.

There has been much speculation in recent years about how the Scriptures came to be written. Very little of the speculation follows the laws of scientific investigation, but unfortunately, it is often presented as fact. It is not. It is speculative theory, and unfortunately can be used by those who wish to take the teeth out of the Scriptures. The second important thing to keep in mind when reading the Gospels is that these words were given to us by the Holy Spirit to guide us on the road to salvation. This fact was confirmed at the Council of Trent.

Christ speaks to us in one way or another in all the books of the Bible. Preeminently He is our teacher in the Gospels. I would enthusiastically suggest a reading every day from the Gospels, with intense concentration and prayer. Such reading does not have to be long, but it must be intense if we are to hear Jesus speaking to us. Then by the grace of God He will become our unique teacher: *unus Magister, Christus.*

Prayer

Take my heart and mind, good Jesus, my teacher and my friend. By Your holy words teach me to follow You, and call me back to the path when I stray from You. Amen.

Wednesday

Behold, we are going up to Jerusalem; and the Son of man will be delivered to the chief priests and scribes, and they will condemn him to death, and deliver him to the Gentiles to be mocked and scourged and crucified, and he will be raised on the third day.

MATTHEW 20:18-19

This text (and you might read the whole passage, Matthew 20:17-28) will open to us the powerful meditation on the passion and Resurrection of Christ. Lent summons us to penance and prayer and other acts of reform. But all this ultimately derives from Our Lord's loving sacrificial gift of Himself on that terrible Passover Friday and His glorious Resurrection on Sunday. This prophecy of His own passion and triumph is so clear that some have speculated that these words were written and, so to speak, put into Jesus' mouth long after the event. Such speculations—and that's all they are—are ultimately unprovable. Anyone who understands scientific investigation knows that it is impossible to prove that something did not happen. The reason for such guessing is ultimately a skepticism about the supernatural—in this case, about Jesus' being able to foretell the future events of His own passion and death. If we choose to be skeptical, then why not doubt the Resurrection itself?

The devout person hearing such speculation may be deprived of the beautiful and haunting drama of the passion, the agony that Jesus of Nazareth truly and knowingly took upon Himself so that you and I might escape eternal death. Every conceivable indication in the Gospels is that Jesus knew exactly what was to come, even as His human nature recoiled before it. Various TV personalities representing skepticism will tell you that Christ was crucified by accident because He was outspoken. They reduce Him to a historical accident. They completely miss the drama of the passion and are left— rather stupidly, I must say—with the question, Why is this innocent holy Person who was killed two thousand years ago still remembered and worshipped by hundreds of millions of people today?

Faith is a gift, but it is also a choice. With God's grace we must accept and cherish this gift. We must press it into our minds and hearts. It opens to us "the mysteries of the kingdom of God" (Mk 4:11; Lk 8:10), as Christ Himself called them. Faith takes us beyond what the mind can know or see and leads us into the mysteries of Christ (Rom 16:25-27). Two thousand years after the events, it seems illogical at the very least to accept some of the biblical accounts of His life and to reject others because they do not fit into the modern, skeptical way of thinking. Cardinal Newman opposed this practice of calling something the word of God and making it the words of men.

Put yourself with the disciples in the Gospel. Your beloved Master, so mysterious and so knowing, someone who never needs to seek the opinion of men but always speaks with authority, tells of His terrifying future. He alludes to the cup of suffering that He is to drink. We all know well enough that great suffering may be just around the corner, but we are able to go on because we do not know when it may come or what form it may take. It might be the death of a loved one or an accident or great failure. But Christ has no such defenses. He lays down His life, as He tells the Pharisees, freely and completely and knowledgeably—"of my own accord" (see Jn 10:17-18). He takes up His Cross for all of us, for each of us, for you and me.

Prayer

Lord Jesus Christ, what can I say to You as You set out on the Via Dolorosa, the Way of Sorrows? Help me to show more gratitude, more respect, more love for You. Write the events of Your passion on my heart so that when my cross comes to me, I may take it up and carry it for You. Amen.

Thursday

If they do not hear Moses and the prophets, neither will they be convinced if someone should rise from the dead.

LUKE 16:31

This remark of Jesus, the concluding line of the parable of Lazarus and the rich man, is filled with Jewish irony. If you grew up with Jewish immigrants from Europe or with any peasant people—Irish, Italian, Slavic, or German—you are familiar with such ironic statements. They are used all the time, and although they are often rhetorical explanations, they always have a message of truth and are meant to shock you out of complacency.

In this verse from St. Luke there may be an allusion to Christ's future Resurrection. Some will debate this, but we will all find out for sure on the other side. In the meantime we might ask ourselves, Are we convinced by someone who has already risen from the dead? Do we take Christ seriously enough in our daily lives? These are very important questions for anyone wishing to be a real Christian, because Christ has said, "If you love me, you will keep my commandments" (Jn 14:15).

If we are to follow the teachings of the One who has risen from the dead, we must face up to several issues. Do I read the words of Christ prayerfully and thoughtfully every day? Am I as familiar as I could be with His specific teaching? Do the following phrases run through my mind: "Love your enemies"; "Do not worry about tomorrow"; "Seek first the kingdom of God"; "Blessed are the poor in spirit." The Gospels are sprinkled with such phrases. There are literally hundreds of commands, counsels, and admonitions we should know and use as guides in everyday life. But Our Lord's words will never guide us unless we know them and ponder them in the light of our own behavior.

Second, do we rationalize or dismiss Jesus' admonitions? Do we simply say, "That does not apply today (or to me), so I don't have to do it"? For instance, Jesus tells His disciples in one place to wear sandals and in another place not to wear them (see Mk 6:9 [sandals]; Mt 10:10; Lk 10:4 [no sandals]). Sandals were the typical footwear of the day, less elegant than boots or slippers (they did not have shoes) and more supportive than going barefoot. Neither sandals nor bare feet may be appropriate in your life, but inexpensive shoes certainly would fulfill the meaning of this admonition.

In the parable of Lazarus and the rich man, Our Lord clearly warns people against superfluity and indicates that the poor suffering beggar is the one who is saved. For those who are well-off, this parable is a warning to live modestly and be generous to the poor. To dismiss the parable merely as a nice story is to allow the seed—the word of God—to fall among the weeds, which will choke any new growth.

All too easily do we dismiss or deny Jesus' words when we should be doing just the opposite. We should be looking through His words eagerly, seeking ways to learn and grow. These are the words of someone who has risen from the dead! I have been around churchy things all my life (I'm sixty years an altar boy), and I have seen the Gospel lived to its fullest by people as different in their positions as

Mother Teresa, Fr. Solanus, and Cardinal Cooke. I've seen it lived by men who worked in Wall Street and by old ladies in Harlem. And I have seen the Gospel ignored completely by people in the same circumstances. The question haunts me: Do I listen to the One who has risen from the dead?

Prayer

Jesus, my teacher and guide, help me to listen to Your words. May I follow these life-giving words with honesty, sincerity, and zeal. May Your holy teaching be spirit and life for me. And when I forget, remind me that You who speak have risen from the dead. Amen.

Friday

The stone which the builders rejected has become the cornerstone.

MATTHEW 21:42

On the Fridays of Lent our thoughts should turn especially ahead to the coming commemoration of the passion of Christ. Our Savior uses these words from Psalm 118:22 to warn His enemies that they are making a very tragic decision by rejecting Him. His parables of the wicked vinedresser who kills the son of the vintner and of the rebellious subjects who refuse to come to the prince's wedding are clear warnings—so clear that His enemies, both the Pharisees and the Sadducees, plotted to kill Him (see all of Mt 22).

To us who live in the ruins of Christian society, it has become commonplace to hear the teachings of Christ rejected and mocked. Because the figure of Jesus of Nazareth is so awesome and inspiring, one rarely hears His enemies attack Him directly. This would be in very bad taste. Rather one of two maneuvers is likely to be used, and the followers of Christ need to be informed of these maneuvers lest, without knowing it, we join in the hostile chorus against Jesus.

The most common maneuver is to attack the teachings of Christ as if they were man-made teachings of the Church. Because many are not familiar enough with the moral teachings of the New Testament, this cheap trick often works, especially in matters of chastity and family values. The second maneuver is more subtle. It is to create a false image of Christ as someone who does not know who he is or what he is doing. One can end up questioning every line in the Gospel, and then one can make a mental snowman and call him Christ. A snowman can be shaped any way its maker wants.

Take the time to get to know the real Jesus—the Jesus of the Gospels—and His words. When those words need interpretation, we should look back to the interpretations of the leaders or Fathers of the early Church. True shepherds of the Church labor and struggle to keep these divine teachings before us. But we ourselves need to make the choice to accept the Son of God or to reject Him, to make His holy teaching a cornerstone or a rock of scandal.

Prayer

Lord Jesus, be my only teacher. Give me the grace to listen to You and to those who prayerfully and without counting the cost seek to know Your teachings which are the words of truth itself. Amen.

Saturday

Let us eat and make merry; for this my son was dead, and is alive again.

LUKE 15:23-24

Rembrandt's very revealing painting of the father's embrace of his repentant child was selected as a logo for the Jubilee Year 2000. This has made the very beautiful and most encouraging parable of the prodigal son much more familiar to Catholics. Almost all thoughtful people see some element of the prodigal son in their own lives, and for many Christians today a return to God from lives of dissipation and sinful behavior is part of their story. It is not surprising that one sees prints of this painting everywhere.

Fellow prodigals, Lent should be our special time. It is a time not only of repentance but also of trust and rejoicing. Anyone with common sense ought to be sorry for moral lapses. We find shame and even penitential acts in all world religions. But there is something very different in Christian repentance, and this unique quality is right there to see in the parable. I suggest you read the passage in St. Luke's Gospel (15:11-32). What is unique?

The son is repentant, but in no way does he earn his father's forgiveness. In fact, his principal motive in returning home is that his wild behavior has led him into misery and starvation. Nevertheless, he comes asking forgiveness, and he is ashamed, as he ought to be. But the forgiveness depends on the father's benevolence, mercy, and compassion.

We are saved by God's grace, which comes to us through the holy life, death, and Resurrection of Jesus Christ—that is, by His obedience. We must accept God's gift of grace and say yes to God.

Nowhere is this acceptance more obvious than in the *fiat* of Mary. She is full of grace. So she can say, "Be it done to me according to Your word." And Christ in His full divine personhood comes to her. But she had to repeat her *fiat* very often in life, especially at Calvary.

We are not full of grace, but we have some. That's why the prodigal son is a model for us. We prodigals need to return to our Father often—every day. I prefer the evening for this. And what joy and peace come from the Father's embrace in prayer and repentance at the end of the day, knowing that Christ has prepared the way for us.

Prayer

Heavenly Father, I come to You again. Let me never forget this loving embrace, which is the beginning of eternal life even now. Let me never be resentful that You have offered that same embrace to everyone else. Amen.

Week Three of Lent

The Third Sunday

Everyone who drinks of this water will thirst again, but whoever drinks of the water that I shall give him will never thirst; the water that I shall give him will become in him a spring of water welling up to eternal life.

JOHN 4:13-14

One of the most mysterious and necessary ingredients of the spiritual life is grace. The account of the Samaritan woman Jesus speaks to at Jacob's well at Sychar can tell us many things about this mysterious grace.

Most informed Christians are fairly clear that there are two distinct kinds of grace. There is the gift of God that prompts us to do good and avoid evil. This prompting may come in dozens of ways, but a bit of personal observation will make it clear that it is a summons to act, and hence it is called actual grace.

But then there is the grace to be, not merely to act. This is a gift of God that makes us His children, living His life, participating in His being so that we will not perish in death or eventually cease to exist, even after some other life beyond this one. Sanctifying grace is, in fact, the gift of eternal life.

In recent decades a number of credible witnesses have reported similar experiences of being alive after they had been pronounced dead, and of later unexpectedly regaining consciousness. These descriptions seem to indicate that there is a life after life, but not the inexpressible and inconceivable experience that is promised by divine grace. These witnesses of life after life seem to be experiencing a continuing journey similar to what Catholics call purgatory.

Whatever one makes of these very fascinating accounts, they do not and, in fact, cannot contain an experience of "what no eye has seen, nor ear heard, nor the heart of man conceived, what God has prepared for those who love him" (1 Cor 2:9). In order to pass from death to the eternal life that Christ promised, we must be united with the source of life, the grace of sanctification, the grace that unites us to the life of God Himself. Because this reality participates in the infinite, it must forever in this life remain a mystery.

But as He often does when it comes to mystery, Our Savior gives us some helpful comparisons or analogies. Just as He compares eternal life to coming home to our Father's house or to a banquet, so He compares grace to a spring of water. This analogy was very powerful to people who lived in the semi-arid Holy Land on the edge of a great desert. Living water! The words themselves are refreshing and exhilarating.

The reality which these comparisons express is a spring of life welling up in us that will continue even when our body dies, when the unity of body and soul is sundered. This is so utterly intriguing and encouraging that no one should ever forget it. An even deeper expression of the reality is that we will begin to live the life of God, for He has told us: "I have come that they may have life and have it more abundantly" (Jn 10:10). This should keep and focus our attention no matter what task we have to do or difficulty we have to endure.

To live in this world with no hope of surviving death is an incredibly dark thought and causes people to hide in bleak denials. The very fabric of our secular society is woven through and through with this denial. Our contemporaries who have no faith cringe even at the thought of death because without faith everything is ultimately of no importance at all. Even believing Christians can get drawn into that denial. But every death we encounter is for a believer a new opportunity to embrace the meaning of our human existence as a preparation for the eternal life to come.

Those who have studied death and dying without faith say that the death of each person we mourn prepares us for our own death. How cheerful! Each death the believer encounters, especially a Christian death, prepares him not for his own death but for his own entrance into eternal life.

To have your life on a truly Christian course, you must embrace the hope of eternal life for yourself, your family, and all whom you love. But you can do this only by facing the frightening reality of the end of earthly life. Once you accept these two things with hope and trust, you will see everything differently. Many of Our Lord's teachings will take on new meaning for you. "I am the resurrection and the life; he who believes in me, though he die, yet shall he live" (Jn 11:25).

Prayer

Lord Jesus, You were crucified, but You overcame death and became Master of life and death. Pour out Your abundant grace on us, that we may live and be witnesses to a life that never ends. Amen.

Monday

Truly, I say to you, no prophet is acceptable in his own country.

LUKE 4:24

The United States was not established as a Christian state but rather as one that welcomed those of many religions. But in spite of its establishment as a secular government, it had for a long time a strong Christian character and culture. This Christian culture appears to have been lost in the last decades of the twentieth century. Surprisingly, several professional polls conducted in the 1990s found among other things that 86 percent of American teenagers identified themselves as Christian and three out of five maintained that the Bible is inerrant. In 2000, George Gallup found that 85 percent of youth saw religion as an important part of their personality.

Despite this, the opinion makers and the media in our country are clearly antireligious and will do anything possible to drive Christian values out of public life. Public figures more sensitive to the polls regularly invoke God and even Christ, but the Supreme Court has restricted religion in public to a very narrow and anemic usage, allowing a very small minority of antireligious people to control public life. The words of Christ apply all too well to the United States and many European countries. Jesus Christ, whose teachings and inspiration were the bedrock of our early settlers, as well as of the armies of immigrants and the freed slaves, is without honor in His own place.

Here is a practice for Lent. Make Christ and His teachings explicit in your life. Let people know what you believe. You can start by wearing a cross or religious symbol. You can mention Christian values in your daily life and identify these as coming from the Bible. Let people know that you are a believer in a way that does not cause offense but makes it clear that freedom of religion does not mean the absence of religion.

When the media are antireligious or undermine Christian values, write and protest explicitly to the sponsors and advertisers of these antireligious programs. Christ has said that He will acknowledge before His heavenly Father all who acknowledge Him before men. You may be inclined to do this in an angry or self-righteous way. Save your peace, and join your protest with prayer for the conversion of those in the media and those who oppose religious practice in our country. Pray even for those who undermine its moral values and for their conversion. Then you will be doing the work of God.

Prayer

Lord Jesus, You have loved me and called out to me. Almost unnoticed, You have saved me from myself. Send me Your Holy Spirit's gift of courage, that I may joyfully and peacefully confess You before all whom I meet. Amen.

Tuesday

Then Peter came up and said to him, "Lord, how often shall my brother sin against me, and I forgive him? As many as seven times?" Jesus said to him, "I do not say to you seven times, but seventy times seven."

MATTHEW 18:21-22

Perhaps the greatest penance of all can be forgiveness, depending on what it is we have to forgive. We have already spoken of the grace to be able to forgive, and have said that forgiveness is a process. First we must decide to forgive and review the reasons for forgiving, beginning with the undeniable fact that God has forgiven us.

In the Gospel cited above, Christ teaches us the necessity of continuing forgiveness. Peter's use of the word *brother* refers to people we know well who may often offend us. A great deal of personal unhappiness of people striving to lead good Christian lives comes from constant friction with loved ones. We feel that others have taken advantage of us or have been ungrateful or hypercritical.

As you make this meditation, think of a couple of people who are permanent sources of pain or annoyance in your life. Don't be surprised if they are also people you love or should love the most—a parent, a spouse, a child, a fellow struggler on the way to Christ. And don't be surprised if some of the things they do are wrong or inconsiderate or even cruel.

But ask yourself why. Every human action has a cause. The cause may be confusion or sickness or a complete distortion or a relapse into total childishness. *C'est la vie*, the French say. That's life. If Jesus Christ was mistreated by His fellowman, if He was betrayed by His apostles and killed by the very people He came to save, don't be surprised if you get hurt by someone you love.

It's wise to pray for guidance, to think over carefully what you are adding to the conflict or what you did to create it in the past, or even how you can help the other person change his or her defensive position toward you. In the worst of circumstances the hurtful person may be twisted or very ill or just unable to be peaceful and livable.

Think this over and you will say to yourself, "I just have to carry this cross, but I will try to carry it with a smile." You will live longer, and when you get to the other side, you will be able to look into the eyes of Jesus and say, "I tried." And perhaps He will say to you, "I know you did."

Prayer

Lord Jesus, give me Your Holy Spirit and His gifts of wisdom, counsel, and courage, that I may forgive with courage, understand with wisdom, and heal with counsel, because You have forgiven me more than seventy times seven. Amen.

Wednesday

Whoever then relaxes one of the least of these commandments and teaches men so, shall be called least in the kingdom of heaven; but he who does them and teaches them shall be called great in the kingdom of heaven.

MATTHEW 5:19

We live in a time when laws, especially religious and moral laws, are ignored and even despised. At the root of this is a rejection of the concept of objective good and evil. Everyone has become his own lawgiver and norm. Sometimes this dismissal of law is even done in the name of conscience. People seem to feel a moral obligation to break an established moral law or at least to express their freedom from it. This may even be thought to be brave.

Nothing could be further from the truth. Conscience is a judgment of reason based on well-considered facts and formed independently of our all too familiar tendency to tell ourselves lies or at least to leave out the truth. Conscience is not a whim or a foolish self-indulgence of passion or greed. A good conscience is informed by God's law. A Christian conscience is further informed by the teaching of Christ in the Gospel and by the Scriptures in general. Often those identified as saints give us insights into the practical living of the law of Christ.

The worst advisers on the observance of Christ's law are those who observe it only on a selective basis, cafeteria-style, and who have no qualms about ignoring particular words of Christ or the teaching of the Church. Often older people like this get nervous when they see the end of the road approaching. But the damage has already been done, and their advisees have gone on blindly and badly confused.

Lent is a good time to ask, Have I bought into the general ignoring of God's law? Or have I omitted what was asked of me? Jesus says, "If you love me, keep my commandments" (Jn 14:15).

Jesus clearly made demands of those who would follow Him. A great Lenten resolution is to take up the Sermon on the Mount (Mt 5–7) and read these demands in one sitting. Read the whole sermon through, and ask yourself if you are observing the law of Christ as best you can. Are you leaving things out? Christ's teachings should be followed carefully with great gratitude and devotion. That's what He means when He says, "If you love me, keep my commandments."

Prayer

Lord Jesus, help me not only to know Your commandments but to keep them as best I can. Help me each day to be a better disciple. Amen.

Thursday

He who is not with me is against me, and he who does not gather with me scatters.

LUKE 11:23

Most of the time in life, when we support someone or go along with someone, we do so with qualifications, and we ought to. No one is perfect. Even if we love people very dearly—a parent, a spouse, or a child—we will do them no good if we can't correct them or at least see when they are wrong.

I've disagreed with people who are now likely to be canonized saints. When I did so, it was very reluctantly, but with an awareness that if I did not disagree, I would be failing them. Everyone needs to hear the truth that he or she may not be aware of. Our Lord disagreed even with His mother on at least two occasions.

But all disagreements and corrections cease when you read the words of Jesus and realize that you are not living up to His expectations of you. Then you are scattering. Often we don't see this. We lack a proper perspective in a given situation, or we are too weak to do what we are called on to do. What should we do when we realize we have scattered?

The simple answer is to admit that we failed and pick up where we are and do better. And this is often the really big stumbling block. We are so afraid to admit that we were wrong or at least wrong-headed that we shy away from the realization that we could have done a lot better. I think this is often a big obstacle on the road to holiness. We don't want to admit that we are in the weeds and off the track.

Get accustomed this Lent to facing up to old mistakes. Maybe we did not do wrong, but we certainly could have done a lot better. This realization may make us depressed, but get beyond your hurt feelings and disappointments.

It's a challenge. The closer we get to God, the more His grace opens our hearts. Then we realize that sometimes we gather with Him and sometimes we scatter. But He is always there to help us if we let Him. Often He is most active when He seems very far away.

Prayer

Lord Jesus, help me to gather with You. I know that I can be very stupid and scatter instead. Help me to be Your more fervent disciple and to give some of Your fire to those whom I love. Amen.

Friday

You shall love the Lord your God with all your heart, and with all your soul, and with all your mind, and with all your strength.... You shall love your neighbor as yourself.

MARK 12:30-31

Love is one of the most ambiguous words we ever use, and yet Our Savior employs it here with such authority and directness that its essential meaning is inescapable to anyone who listens to Him carefully.

At best in modern times love has come to mean emotional dependency and a corresponding affectionate and caring response to the beloved. In simpler times love was more practical. Far less emphasis was placed on affection, especially the expression of affection, which like all emotional states can be very unstable and unpredictable.

In the time of Our Lord and during most of human history, especially among the great masses of people who were farmers, hunters, and fishermen, or later artisans and craftsmen, and among clergy and religious, love meant faithfully fulfilling one's duties to another, seeing to their welfare, and providing for their needs. *Facta, non verba* (Deeds, not words) was a popular saying that summed up love.

In Scripture, which is written by and immediately directed to the vast majority of people, not to aristocracy and their retainers like the poets and writers, love means deeds. "Not what we say but what we do." I do not mean to disparage in any way the linking of affection and tender emotion with fidelity to and practical concern for the one who is loved. Such a union of deeds and affection probably represents a positive development in human history. I say probably because in fact there was much more fidelity, much more commitment to spouse, family, friends, a religious community or movement, even to one's own nation and people, before affective expression was seen as so important.

Whatever love means now, it once meant fidelity, generous concern, and joyful giving of self. That's what it means when in the Scriptures we are called to love God and our neighbor. We see the highest expression of love in Christ's obedience to the Father's will that He drink the cup of human suffering and do always "the will of Him who sent me." We see His love for human beings, His neighbors, in His whole life of self-giving, His compassion, His work among the poor and sick.

The argument between Catholics and Orthodox Christians on one side and some Protestants on the other over faith and works would have made little or no sense to people before the Renaissance, which emphasized affective love. Before that time faith and love of God were not seen as different expressions, and they jointly called for doing something, for fidelity and generous concern.

In that early sense in which Our Savior spoke, Do I love God and my neighbor? Am I faithful, reliable, responsive? Do I give my all, or even want to give my all? Do I simply want to get the minimum done, fulfill the barest responsibility?

If an honest friend looked at me and my life, could that person say that I love the Lord with all my heart, soul, mind, and strength, and my neighbor as myself? Or am I just giving enough to pass? How beautiful is a life of fidelity, dedication, and generosity. How dull and depressing is anything else.

Prayer

Lord, give me the grace to love and to love more—not to love myself but to be ever more faithful, generous, and giving, not looking for a reward. Amen.

Saturday

For every one who exalts himself will be humbled, but he who humbles himself will be exalted.

LUKE 18:14

A certain kind of humility, modesty in the presentation of self, motivated by an equally modest assessment of one's own abilities and virtues, is counseled by most of the religions of the world, except the most immature forms of paganism. In fact, the paganism that Christianity encountered and replaced was not a religion of modesty. But there was and still is strong recognition of the value of modesty and humility in both Buddhism and Hinduism, as well as the Shinto tradition. Islam and, even more so, Judaism share the revelation of the divinely approved virtue of humility.

Regrettably, it must also be stated that in all these religions, Christianity included, humility can be easily forgotten and over-looked. The religions of the world have in common high priests, preachers, teachers, gurus, and significant personages who trade modesty for religious importance. This is because we all have pride in our hearts. There is the other side, too—humble popes, modest preachers, devout teachers who make little of things like importance. You cannot look at the honest history of any religion without finding the humble and the exalted. If you look closely, you will find the exalted who are really humble and, apparently, even the humble who have the pride of an emperor.

Our Savior, continuing the biblical tradition, puts strong empha-sis on humility and the truest foundation of humility—the self before God. We find that He seems to have a special predilection for sinners. He goes to their houses as a guest, He saves their lives when they are threatened with capital punishment, He accepts their homage all the time, calling them—and everyone else—to repentance and conver-sion. And even though He identifies Himself as the Son of God, which is the highest and most exalted nobility, He accepts a humili-ation proportionate in depth to the loftiness of His heavenly dignity.

Human society today is not lacking in public officials; in fact, they are riding rather high. Christ's disciple, following the Master's ex-ample, must show them due respect; he must render to Caesar the things that are Caesar's. Remember, the publican in this parable was a quisling, a Jew who had sold out to the Romans and who made his living gouging extra taxes from them. He was an apostate. His marriage was not recognized nor the legitimacy of his family. He could not go into the parts of the temple reserved for the Jews. He was far worse than a pagan; he was a traitor. And Jesus chose to tell the parable about this humble publican. There are several groups of people in our society whose lifestyle the devout Christian must recognize as sinful and morally unacceptable. But according to this parable, they, like the publican, may be received with dignity and called gently to conversion if they approach the Lord with humility and truth. Don't worry too much about them. Worry about you and me, that we who do pray may not pray like the Pharisee.

Prayer

Lord Jesus, give me some of Your boundless humility. You may have to let me suffer. You may have to let me learn the hard way. But let me learn. Jesus, meek and humble of heart, make my heart like Yours. Amen.

Week Four of Lent

The Fourth Sunday

Jesus said, "For judgment I came into this world, that those who do not see may see, and that those who see may become blind." Some of the Pharisees near him heard this, and they said to him, "Are we also blind?" Jesus said to them, "If you were blind, you would have no guilt; but now that you say, 'We see,' your guilt remains."

JOHN 9:39-41

The intriguing account of the healing of the man born blind is, from a human point of view, one of the most revealing passages in the Gospels. With great detail we see how people think not only about Christ's miracles but also about life itself. The obvious goal of the passage is to communicate that this healing was to demonstrate the desire of Jesus to work miracles or, to use the language of the Bible, to do marvelous things by the hand of God.

But woven into the account is Christ's teaching about His being the Light of the world. More than once He refers to Himself unequivocally as the transcending Light. John calls Him the light which enlightens everyone who comes into the world (Jn 1:9). Another mystery.

At the end of the narrative of the healing, Christ Himself takes up the theme of His being the Light of the world. He does this in a confrontational way with those who witness His miracles and signs and whose hardness of heart does not permit them to believe and acknowledge Him. He tells them that they who see have become blind, and because they don't admit it, they sin and their sin remains.

Why did they not accept Jesus of Nazareth when they were the witnesses of so many wonderful signs—His many healings and even His restoration of the dead to life? They were religious people. They certainly accepted the possibility of miraculous healing, since such healings take place in the Jewish Scriptures. Presumably, many of those who rejected Jesus Christ were not Sadducees, who for the most part denied the supernatural and miracles; those who rejected Him tended to be Pharisees, who accepted miraculous signs of God's approval.

In his simplicity, the cured blind man asked them if they were going to become disciples of Christ because He had restored the sight of someone blind from birth. Why did they not become His disciples? Why instead did they react with rage and threaten him? Good questions.

Because it would have been difficult, inconvenient, humiliating, even dangerous, for them to suddenly accept this wonder-working prophet and His outrageous claim about His relationship to God.

A few of their number did in fact come to believe. We know of Joseph of Arimathea and Nicodemus, who buried Him, but they were secret disciples. But looking back at the whole drama of the conflict between Christ and the Pharisees and scribes, a conflict that brought Him to Calvary, we can be astounded that intelligent human beings could reject the eternal Son of God, the Incarnate Word, because they would be inconvenienced or even endangered. But that's what happened! And it still happens.

The question now is, How many refuse to look at Christ, to take Him seriously, even to read a Gospel, before they decide to drop out of the practice of their faith? How many politicians and would-be leaders deny both the Ten Commandments and the whole teaching of Christ to get elected to some office? How many believing Christians and even clergy symbolically come to Christ by night, like Nicodemus? They don't open their mouths about many evils that call out to God for judgment.

And finally—and this is the point of this meditation—how often do you and I fail to bear witness to Him when it involves some inconvenience or embarrassment, however slight? I say that I see, but am I blind to the presence of Christ in so many ways in daily life because it will cost me something—some inconvenience, embarrassment, or rejection? St. Paul said we ought to be glad to suffer for Him who suffered so much for us. When we see this, then we see.

Prayer

Lord Jesus Christ, Light of the world, be my guiding light at all times. Help me to recognize when I choose the shadows, even the darkness, and let me cherish the Light of the world which You are. Amen.

March 19[1]

St. Joseph

Now the birth of Jesus Christ took place in this way. When his mother Mary had been betrothed to Joseph, before they came together she was found to be with child of the Holy Spirit; and her husband Joseph, being a just man and unwilling to put her to shame, resolved to send her away quietly. But as he considered this, behold, an angel of the Lord appeared to him in a dream, saying, "Joseph, son of David, do not fear to take Mary your wife, for that which is conceived in her is of the Holy Spirit; she will bear a son, and you shall call his name Jesus, for he will save his people from their sins."... When Joseph woke from sleep, he did as the angel of the Lord commanded him.

MATTHEW 1:18-21; 24

In recent centuries Catholics have shown a special devotion to that providentially chosen man who was to protect the Christ Child and His mother. Though we do not know much about St. Joseph from the Scriptures, we know enough to make him a very endearing

---

[1]The day, though not the date, of this feast will change each year. The reader is asked to make the appropriate adjustment in using this meditation.

saint. He was chosen by God Himself for a very mysterious and demanding role. Neither priest nor scholar, Joseph is accurately described in the New Testament as a construction worker (a *tekton*).

The most important thing about him is that he does what he is told without question or personal consideration. He travels to Egypt along roads patrolled only by murderous robbers. He asks no questions. He comes back to Nazareth and has to cope with the most mysterious boy who ever lived. Joseph also silently goes through the loss of the Christ Child and, after three days' searching, hears the mysterious response, "Did you not know that I had to be about My Father's business?"

Then Joseph just disappears in the long, silent years of almost two decades. We are not given any facts about Christ's life during this time. Popular devotion has made St. Joseph, logically enough, the patron of a happy death, deriving from the fact that he is not mentioned in the public life of Jesus and therefore must have died before it began.

Also logically, St. Joseph is seen as a model of chastity—in his case, of complete sexual abstinence. Ancient writers describe him as a widower, and Michelangelo left a sketch, now in the Vatican Museum, of Joseph with his own children standing next to Mary and the Christ Child. In modern times he has been seen as the virginal, chaste young man.

Devout attention to this silent, chosen, just, and faithful man has plenty of justification. An imperfect mortal man, he lived with the effects of original sin in a household of perfect people. The Child entrusted to him was a divine Person, and his wife, full of grace, was redeemed like us all but in a singular way that left her without the effects of original sin, like moral weakness and ignorance.

What were his responses? Fidelity, justice, humility, and an unquestioning obedience to God. No wonder so very many people make him a patron saint or a spiritual friend, myself included. And every layperson earning his or her daily bread, doing God's will as best he or she can, every blue- and white-collar worker, speaks to me of St. Joseph.

Prayer

Heavenly Father, You have shared your fatherhood with so many parents—mothers and fathers. You invite us all to serve Your Son in the example of Joseph, that we may, with faith and humility, do Your will. Amen.

Monday

The man believed the word that Jesus spoke to him and went his way.

JOHN 4:50

How many times do we ask God for something very good, even apparently very necessary? It is part of being a believer—to ask and to trust. And often enough we do not receive precisely what we ask for, at least at the time we ask for it. But the believing Christian, looking back over life with all its failures, disappointments, miseries, and sorrows, will realize that God did indeed hear our prayers and responded to them in ways that are far more beneficial, at least when seen in the light of eternity.

The royal official whose son or servant boy was dying humbly put his trust in Jesus, whom he knew only as an itinerant preacher and healer. And his prayer was wonderfully answered in the very hour he asked for help.

On the other hand, it would seem that the Blessed Virgin must have prayed that her Son would be safe after He was arrested. Surely the holy women who accompanied Jesus on Good Friday prayed that the torture would stop. And yet He was crucified before their eyes. Were their prayers heard? Yes, they were indeed heard, and in a way that was inconceivable to them at the time they prayed in horror, seeing Jesus beaten and crowned with thorns.

There is much to be learned here. When we pray for something we need, even desperately, we must still struggle to put our trust in Jesus and His promise that we will be heard. His response, like a miracle of healing, may be what we asked for. Or we may not receive the answer we had hoped for.

The person we cherish and need so very much may, in fact, be taken away from us instead of being healed. It is the person's hour to pass from this valley of tears. Someday we may see this tragedy lead to good things, even if the death was the result of the wickeness of men, as was the death of Christ. God will bring good out of evil, and we may be a part of this victory even if we do not know it. But it is always a test of faith. We must put our trust in the words that Jesus spoke to us.

Prayer

Holy Spirit, fill my heart with faith in Jesus Christ, in His presence and providence acting in my life today. Let me have this trust even in dark times, the kind of trust that Jesus requires. Amen.

Tuesday

See, you are well! Sin no more, that nothing worse befall you.

JOHN 5:14

The touching healing of the paralytic at the pool of Bethsaida is, of course, another occasion on which Jesus healed on the sabbath, making people look at their priorities. He wanted them to realize that the sabbath was made for man and not the reverse.

But there is something else to be learned: Christ asks for repentance and conversion. We know nothing about this paralytic except that he had been waiting a long time to be healed. Presumably Christ knew him better, because He tells him to sin no more, as He did in the case of His first miracle with another paralytic in Mark 2:1-12.

In our pagan times it is worthwhile to recall clearly and often that Our Lord calls us to repentance. He does this because He is the Holy One, the Sinless One, before whom each of us is to appear at the moment we leave this world.

Only fifty years ago the vast majority of people who lived in the United States and in the rest of the Christian world did not question this fact, which is made eminently clear by Christ in the Gospels and in the whole Bible. There was hardly any respected theologian who did not see Christ's moral teaching as well as the reality of the divine reckoning as essential themes of the Christian life. As it says in the "Battle Hymn of the Republic," "He is sifting out the hearts of men before His judgment seat."

What has happened? A widespread moral relativism has taken over, with or without attempts at theological and scriptural justification. This relativism can be observed in many sermons, especially at funerals. While it is improper to recount the moral shortcomings of the deceased in the funeral sermon, it is also presumptuous to eulogize the person as if he or she were one of the saints in heaven. This presumption of heavenly glory is no help to the deceased, because it can deprive him or her of the prayers they need, and it can be absolutely harmful to the thoughtless and uninformed who listen.

Jesus Christ said, "Give up your sins." He meant it!

Prayer

Lord Jesus, let me know each day how I can follow You better. Help me avoid sin when I see it coming and overcome temptations when they are there. Teach my heart what I am to do, and help me to be a good example to all I meet. Amen.

Wednesday

Jesus answered them, "My Father is working still, and I am working.... Truly, truly, I say to you, the Son can do nothing of his own accord, but only what he sees the Father doing; for whatever he does, that the Son does likewise. For the Father loves the Son, and shows him all that he himself is doing."

JOHN 5:17, 19-20

This is one of the most intriguing passages in St. John's Gospel. In glowing words he gives us teachings about Our Savior that burn with the light of eternity. In chapter after chapter Jesus Christ speaks of His divine origin, of His relationship of equality with the Father, and especially of the mutual love of the Father and the Son.

It is a foundational principle of the Christian faith that the Scriptures are inspired by the Holy Spirit, that they are without error and the words of God, even though they also have human authors who are intelligent instruments of His inspiration. The divine inspiration and inerrancy of Sacred Scripture have been defined dogmas of the Church from the early centuries and are believed by serious Christians of all persuasions.

In recent decades the skepticism of the European Enlightenment, which denied the supernatural and the possibility of the Incarnation as understood by Christianity, crept into the various denominations. Wishing to respond to this challenge, some scholars made unwarranted concessions that ultimately led to the denial of the divine personhood of Jesus of Nazareth. Any honest person reading the Gospels, especially that of John, must admit herein He proclaims Himself equal to the Father. In fact, that is why His enemies put Him to death. He "called God his Father, making himself equal with God" (Jn 5:18).

You may have heard all sorts of attempts to reconcile the two points of view—faith and a rationalist prejudice against the supernatural. Pope John Paul II has said that it is a scandal that denials of the faith can be taught under the name of Christianity. He was referring to a truncated vision of the divinity of Christ, according to which Christ did not know who He was and performed no miracles, and even His Virgin Birth and Resurrection are myths.

Lent is a time for acts of faith, hope, and love. Can you believe in someone who does not even know who he is, hope in someone who works no signs and wonders by the power of God, and love someone who may not even know that you exist? During these weeks before Easter we will often read from the Gospel of John. Read this sublime, inspired writing on your knees, in silent adoration of the mysterious presence who steps off the page to embrace the soul that comes to Him to find rest—a rest no other can give.

Prayer

Lord Jesus, open to me the streams of life contained in the words of the Gospel. Show me that You have revealed Yourself in the Gospels and in all of Scripture. Fill me with the word of life so that I may share it with others. Amen.

Thursday

But the testimony which I have is greater than that of John; for the works which the Father has granted me to accomplish, these very works which I am doing, bear me witness that the Father has sent me. And the Father who sent me has himself borne witness to me. His voice you have never heard, his form you have never seen.... You search the scriptures because you think that in them you have eternal life; and it is they that bear witness to me; yet you refuse to come to me that you may have life.

JOHN 5:36-37, 39-40

These powerful words of Jesus follow on the account of the cure of the paralytic at the pool. It's interesting that His critics, the very enemies who would seek His death, did not attempt to deny that He had cured this man, as they had done in the case of the man born blind. They rather absurdly clung to their usual objection that He cured on the sabbath.

It is very important to see that Jesus refers to His works as testimony to His union with the Father. One thing that His disciples and His enemies agreed on is that He expressly used His miracles to prove His unprecedented claims to have come forth from the Father. "I came from the Father and have come into the world; again, I am leaving the world and going to the Father" (Jn 16:28).

Those ancient Scripture commentators, the Fathers of the Church, constantly appeal to Christ's signs and wonders to prove His divinity. They did not miss the irony that the person who did these things Himself suffered humiliation and death, that He who saved others did not save Himself—an echo of the taunt thrown up to Him as He was dying on the Cross.

Even apart from the testimony that these supernatural acts give— signs and wonders as varied as healing the terminally ill, raising the dead, and calming the wind and the sea—there is something else revealed here, something precious and most mysterious. With our limited human minds we can only stand in the light of this mystery. Jesus makes it clear that He is not the Father in human form. People have made that mistake in the past and have said that the Father suffered and died on Calvary.

Jesus even has a will, a human will, distinct from the Father's. "I seek not my own will but the will of him who sent me" (Jn 5:30). Obviously, since there can be only one divine will, Christ in His complete human nature also has a human body, soul, memory, intelligence, and will. This would be the constant teaching of the early Church councils and would be shared by Catholics, Orthodox Christians, and later, the early Protestants. Jesus also tells us that He and the Father are one (Jn 10:30) and that He has come forth from the Father. John proclaims Him to be the Word of God who is God (Jn 1:1).

Is Jesus of Nazareth, then, two persons—the divine Son of God and the human Son of Mary? The Council of Ephesus (431) taught that the divine Person holds His divine nature and human nature in a single union, which is called hypostatic, because it is a union in person.

Think about this Person. Unlike any other miracle worker, including Sts. Peter and Paul, God does not only work through Him. The Son shares the life of the Father and all His power. "For as the Father has life in himself, so he has granted the Son also to have life in himself" (Jn 5:26).

It is wise in our days of theological confusion to prayerfully consider the ancient teachings of the Church and to let them guide you and what you think about Jesus Christ. Reflect, for example, on these words of St. Augustine:

The Lord Jesus, the only begotten of the Father and co-eternal with the Creator, equally invisible, equally immutable, equally omnipotent, equally God, for us ... was made man, taking upon Himself human shape without losing His divinity, with His power now hidden and appearing in weakness.... He was born that we might be reborn, died that we might not die forever.... On the third day He rose again.... He showed Himself that He might be seen by the disciples and touched by their hands; convincing them of what He had become but not relinquishing what He always was. He kept company with them for forty days ... coming and going, eating and drinking, no longer now because of need but in His full power, and manifesting to them the truth of His flesh, its weakness on the Cross and its immortality beyond the sepulchre (Sermon 262, I).

Prayer

Father, give me Your Holy Spirit that I may believe and know, as best I can, that Jesus is Son of Mary and Son of God. Amen.

Friday

So Jesus proclaimed, as he taught in the temple, "You know me, and you know where I come from? But I have not come of my own accord; he who sent me is true, and him you do not know. I know him, for I come from him, and he sent me."

JOHN 7:28-29

How stupid the institutions of men can be. After all His signs and wonders, after all His preaching and works of love, Jesus must cry out in the temple that He is the One who is sent, and few take Him seriously. And fewer still believe.

The Jewish religion was the religion of God, but it expressed itself on earth in the human institution made up primarily of the clergy, scribes, and Pharisees. They could be stupid. The Church is also a work of God, but the human institutions that are part of it in this world can also be stupid.

You may think it's different now. A billion Catholics, hundreds of millions of Orthodox Christians, and more hundreds of millions of Protestants believe in Christ. Oh, yeah? A few years ago I was invited by Cardinal Christoph Schönborn, the brilliant and fervent archbishop of Vienna, to preach a clergy retreat in Austria. When he asked me my topic, I answered, "Devotion to Jesus Christ." He replied that I could not have chosen a better topic, "because Christ has all but disappeared in northern Europe."

For years the most influential voice in the study of the Bible was the German pastor named Rudolf Bultmann. You may never have heard his name, but I suspect you have heard his teachings. Writing from his own experience with his own method, Bultmann said that the more we study the figure of Jesus, the more remote He becomes.

Each year before Christmas and Easter the Jesus Seminar presents Bultmann's ideas as gospel truth on public television. The Jesus Seminar out-Bultmanns Bultmann. I have long believed that it requires only moderate intelligence to be moderately stupid, but to be very stupid requires great intelligence.

Institutions of men remain as potentially stupid as they ever were. Despite its divine origin and Christ's promise to guide the Church, the human part of Christianity has managed many times to be just as stupid as everybody else. A number of saints like Augustine, Jerome, and Catherine of Siena, and in modern times Cardinal Newman, have seen this rather clearly. How does an ordinary believer avoid denying or giving only lip service to Christ's clear teaching that He has come from God to earn our salvation and show us how to follow Him so that He can give it to us? How can Christians keep the true Christ before them as their God?

One way is to fall on your knees, embrace His presence, listen to His voice in your heart, and express your desperate need for Him. Then you will know that He is the Son of God.

Prayer

O Christ, be my only teacher and my true life. Then I will hear only those who speak truly of You, and I will embrace that light that comes only from You. Amen.

Saturday

Some said, "Is the Christ to come from Galilee? Has not the scripture said that the Christ is descended from David, and comes from Bethlehem, the village where David was?" "Search and you will see that no prophet is to rise from Galilee."

JOHN 7:41-42, 52

Galilee was the boondocks. It was not merely rural or what urban people call the sticks. It was remote and half-pagan but was also home to observant, simple, loyal Jews. The half-pagan city of Sephoris, less than five miles from Nazareth, had been extensively rebuilt over a period of years. It seems quite likely that Joseph, a *tekton* or construction worker (carpenter, mason, and laborer altogether), and his son would probably have found work there. People from Galilee had rural accents.

As a city boy, I'm uncomfortable with all of this. Despite a thousand lessons that life has taught me about rural and country people, I sometimes still have urban prejudices. City dwellers, especially New Yorkers, know well enough that people from country places can be wise, conscientious, loving, and much more sensitive than we are. But we think they are not savvy, or street-smart. Woe, the prophets and saints and the Messiah Himself did not come from the city, but they frequently were killed there. We savvy city kids can be deplorably stupid because we are wrapped up in our own phony wisdom. Street smarts are no substitute for wisdom.

Was this meditation written only for city slickers? No. Here comes the punch. Television and the Internet have made everybody savvy with the foolishness of the world. The media form a world of make-believe, and only fools believe in it. Even when the media attempt to present the message of Christ, they usually do a bad job. (I do know a cloistered nun with a TV network who does a much better job. But Mother Angelica is a city girl.)

Even great music and great art, which the media seldom employ, cannot lead to Christ, although they can express faith and be offered as an act of homage to Him. Unfortunately, this is done rarely enough.

The fact is that Christ must be known in the simplicity of faith, by the shore of the lake and in the city street, in the company of the poor and the sick. He must be found in the reality of the desperateness of the human situation, which no street smarts or sophistication can ever really appreciate. In His presence the city boy and the farmer, the sophisticate and the fisherman's wife, all fall to silence on their knees and realize that no one has ever spoken like this man before, and no one ever can again.

Prayer

Lord Jesus, give us the grace to escape our own self-importance and leave aside all earthly things, because You, the King of all, are here. Amen.

March 25[1]

Annunciation Day

And the angel said to her, "Do not be afraid, Mary, for you have found favor with God. And behold, you will conceive in your womb and bear a son, and you shall call his name Jesus. He will be great, and will be called the Son of the Most High; and the Lord God will give to him the throne of his father David, and he will reign over the house of Jacob for ever; and of his kingdom there will be no end." And Mary said to the angel, "How can this be, since I have no husband?" And the angel said to her, "The Holy Spirit will come upon you, and the power of the Most High will overshadow you; therefore the child to be born will be called holy, the Son of God."

LUKE 1:30-35

Recently a science magazine displayed on its cover an object about the size of a hazelnut with the caption, "The universe at 10^{t24} power (actual size)." This is the theory about the origin of the universe, namely, that it began with an object that small. Actually, it's a

---

[1]If March 25 falls in Passiontide, the feast is moved to the Monday following the Easter octave.

bit inaccurate. We who have the Bible know that it began with nothing. But science can't go back that far.

The explosion of the entire universe from that little object is what is called a singularity, that is, an event that can happen only once in the history of time. There are two other singularities that we know of from divine revelation. One is the Resurrection, and the other is the Incarnation of the Son of God, which we commemorate on the Feast of the Annunciation.

At the Annunciation something took place that never occurred before or can again. The divine became linked in union with the human. A divine Person came to live in the passing world of humanity, which emerged from the explosion of that tiny object at the beginning of time. Eternity and time were joined in a union that would never, ever end—that is, in the risen body of Our Lord Jesus Christ. In the next singularity to occur, the Resurrection, we see that Christ's human body, a part of this passing world, is so linked with the divine Person that His human body will last forever.

The Feast of the Annunciation is a day of great mystery. Almost every important artist of Western civilization has pictured this event. I particularly find great meaning in the painting by America's first great black artist, Henry Oswana Tanner, which now hangs in the Philadelphia Museum of Art. In this beautiful painting Tanner, whose father was a bishop of one of the first black churches, depicts the archangel as a shaft of shimmering, living light, rather than as a human person. After you study it for a while, you realize that the Blessed Virgin, looking on with a mixture of joy, fear, anticipation, and humility, has the face of Our Lady of Guadalupe, with which

Tanner would have been familiar. What a magnificent thing it is to remember that this singularity of the Incarnation took place in a tiny peasant village, in a very modest home, to a young Jewish girl who nobody thought was different except God.

In the midst of Lent we always stop on Annunciation day to rejoice, to say the Gloria, to lift up our hearts, and to recall this other singular event. None of this would have ever happened unless God had come to us and the Word had been made flesh.

As we prepare for the celebration of Holy Week, it is probably very wise to go back and review the Incarnation and birth of Christ. The Annunciation and Christmas, along with Good Friday, focus on the humanity of Christ while never denying His divinity. It's important to keep the humanity in front of us in Holy Week so we'll understand how, although He was God, He was able to suffer with us.

Prayer

Lord Jesus Christ, we celebrate Your entrance into our dark world, a world of pain and difficulty, even of death. You came here for us that we might one day enter into Your world, a world of everlasting life, where there is neither mourning nor crying, nor weeping anymore. Amen.

Week Five of Lent

Passion Sunday

And Jesus lifted up his eyes and said, "Father, I thank thee that thou hast heard me. I knew that thou hearest me always, but I have said this on account of the people standing by, that they may believe that thou didst send me." When he had said this, he cried with a loud voice, "Lazarus, come out!" The dead man came out, his hands and feet bound with bandages, and his face wrapped with a cloth. Jesus said to them, "Unbind him, and let him go."

JOHN 11:41-44

The raising of Lazarus—along with Jesus' dialogue with the apostles and later with Mary, in which He makes clear that He is not only the One who is to come but also the Resurrection and the Life—is an astonishing episode in an already astounding life. The account should be read here and now in its entirety (see Jn 11:1-45).

The evangelist has made credible the incredible by so many details and especially by the unexpected description of Christ's becoming deeply emotionally distressed. Since the text indicates that Christ intended to restore the dead brother to his sisters, why was He so troubled? Perhaps it's simply a sympathy and tenderness at seeing the grief of His friends.

It goes without saying that those who have trouble with miracles frequently get off the train before it ever arrives at Bethany. They will deny that Lazarus was raised from the dead, but they were not there. I would rather take seriously the wise and thoughtful author of St. John's Gospel than accept the denials of outright skeptics or the theories of those who hope to dialogue with them.

What is the most obvious meaning of this account, along with the other two events where Christ calls someone back from the dead—the little girl and the widow's son? The message is that Jesus Christ is Lord of life and death. Did He not have to make this at least partially clear even before His own passion and death?

The apostles lived at a time when ghosts were taken quite seriously. The risen Christ was not a ghost or a specter or even a vision (Lk 24:39). He made those who saw Him realize that He had flesh and bone (Lk 24:35). He even ate a fish and some honey (Lk 24:43).

Death, the universal frustration and irreversible catastrophe of all human life, is not that to Him. He apparently used the death of the widow's son, that of the little girl, and, finally, that of Lazarus to prove that death is no obstacle to Him. He would die, but death would not hold Him.

What about death, the death of someone dear to us, someone we need or admire or love? This is where faith comes in.

Rather than playing games with Scripture and putting my faith in a lot of flimsy theories, I prefer to take the inspired word of God simply as the truth. The raising of the three dead people actually happened, according to those who were there. And it is not at all incredible if you believe that Jesus Christ is Master of life and death, because He is the Way, the Truth, and the Life.

I'd quit being a Christian and take my chances on the general hope that the human race has had for millennia that death is not the end rather than call myself a disciple of Christ and play around with the Resurrection. Those who can't accept the accounts of Jesus' raising of Lazarus, the little girl, and the widow's son, all told with such remarkable detail, are going to have even greater difficulty with the glorious Resurrection. These events are all recorded by the same sources.

The raising of Lazarus is steeped in mystery with many unanswerable questions. Yet this mystery the mind can deal with. The Resurrection of Jesus by His own divine power and His Ascension back to God are beyond all human understanding. They do not contradict human reason; they go beyond where it can go. They bring us to the edge of the infinite sea of God's life. All is divine mystery, unfathomable and inscrutable.

The raising of Lazarus, so close in time to Christ's own Resurrection, was a preparation for the events to come. But the risen Lazarus is far different from the risen Christ. Lazarus died again, and his body and soul will be reunited on the last day. Jesus rose and will never die again and will call us all at death and on the last day. The mind alone cannot deal adequately with these things. If Christ did not rise from the dead, why does anyone even remember His name?

Prayer

Christ Jesus, Lord of life and death, give me Your Holy Spirit to keep always before my soul the faith in Your Resurrection, the reflection of the light of endless day, which we shall see when we are with You in Your Father's house. Amen.

Monday

Jesus looked up and said to her, "Woman, where are they? Has no one condemned you?" She said, "No one, Lord." And Jesus said, "Neither do I condemn you; go, and do not sin again."

JOHN 8:10-11

In our meditations so far we have seen that Jesus Christ not only called people to observe the moral law, the law of God, but He called them to an ever greater and more mature following of God's will. He calls us all to walk on the straight way and enter by the narrow gate, and also to love God with all our heart, soul, mind, and strength.

Yet we also know that He is most compassionate and forgiving to sinners, that He has, in fact, the forgiving mind of God. This makes Him the Lamb of God who takes away the sins of the world. He does not simply dismiss sin, as we might do with the misbehavior of children. He atones for sin and forgives it explicitly on Calvary.

There are a few sins which perturbed Jesus, especially when the sinner was not penitent: self-righteousness, pride, judgment of others' moral weaknesses, and a judgmental attitude in general. He also expressed great displeasure at hardness of heart and the failure to accept His Gospel, which He had backed up by numerous miraculous signs. Then there is the scandalizing of the young and the sin against the Holy Spirit.

The woman in today's Gospel, as well as the woman at the well and the woman with the alabaster jar of ointment (usually identified as Mary Magdalene), all received kindly and forgiving treatment. Despite the fact that Christ's teaching on sexual morality given in the Sermon on the Mount is the most demanding, He was gentle with all three sexual sinners we meet in the Gospel. In fact, He saved the poor woman taken in adultery from a terrible death by stoning.

The fact that all three who received His kindness were women may very well be seen as His rejection of the injustice of the double standard, which was so obviously biased against women. It is worth noting that throughout the Gospel, women are far more receptive to Jesus than men, and they are loyal to Him to the end.

For forty years as a priest I have worked with the poor and with at least a couple of thousand women who would be seen by the world as unrespectable. Not one of these women was ever disrespectful or forward in any way. I always was deeply moved by the way these poor women had been mistreated.

Much of what Jesus Christ does is mysterious, but this is not. He is compassionate, but He also says, "Go, and do not sin again." You might be surprised to learn how many poor women I know who later on came to lead holy and penitent lives.

Prayer

Lord Jesus, help me not to judge, not to be severe, most of all not to be self-righteous. Teach me to be compassionate and to try always to help the other person come closer to God. Amen.

Tuesday

When you have lifted up the Son of man, then you will know that I am he, and that I do nothing on my own authority but speak thus as the Father taught me. And he who sent me is with me; he has not left me alone, for I always do what is pleasing to him.

JOHN 8:28-29

This remarkable passage, in which Jesus Christ indicates His death, as He does several times, is so prophetic that scholars of a more rationalist bent of mind will claim that these and many other words in St. John's Gospel were written after Jesus' death. The scholars, however, were not present at the time, and the fact is that these words are given to the believing Christian as the word of God inspired by the Holy Spirit to guide us on our way to eternity. The real question is, What do these inspired words of the Holy Spirit mean?

To the ears of the believer they are yet another and even clearer instance of Jesus of Nazareth's preaching His divinity, His equality with the Father. The use of the words "I am," the divine name, make this clear. But they also manifest His real humanity. He speaks of the Father's teaching Him, remaining with Him, and not deserting Him. These are words that indicate humanity—an utterly unique humanity, but a human relationship with God nonetheless.

These mysterious words, like the words He spoke in Gethsemane, "Not my will but your will be done," and on the Cross, "Why have you forsaken me?" remind us that Jesus Christ also had a human nature. Centuries later the Church Fathers—in seven ecumenical councils spread over more than three hundred years—would wrestle with these texts to come to some coherent, if partial, understanding of the relationship of humanity and divinity in the mysterious figure of the most singular human being who ever lived.

They would decide, in complete agreement with the whole of the Bible, that He had both human and divine natures, and that He could experience things like other men—things like pain, conflict, and even human death. And yet He was divine, one with the Father. He could operate completely in two natures: one divine, eternal, and unfathomable, and the other human and one with ours. The Fathers also taught unequivocally and in the face of endless opposition that the Person of Jesus Christ was divine, not human. As Son of God, He always was, is, and ever shall be. As Son of man, he could be lifted up on the sacrificial gibbet of the Cross; He could suffer, be in agony, and die the death that we all fear.

Think about it. St. Augustine reminds us that we gave to Him through His Blessed Mother what as God He did not have: the capacity to die. And He gave us what we do not have as human beings: a capacity to live forever.

Prayer

Lord Jesus, always in the depths of my heart, be lifted up so that You may draw me to Yourself. Amen.

Wednesday

Jesus then said to the Jews who had believed in him, "If you continue in my word, you are truly my disciples, and you will know the truth, and the truth will make you free.... If God were your Father, you would love me, for I proceeded and came forth from God; I came not of my own accord, but he sent me."

JOHN 8:31-32, 42

We have already meditated in these pages on truth—beautiful, powerful, transforming truth. And we have seen that in our age when the media spew out lies and untruth, we hardly know what truth is. It is not simply an agreement between reality and our description of that reality in words or thoughts. That might be called descriptive or verbal truth, and it is rare enough. But there is a deeper truth that exists without being described. It is the truth of existence. It is how things really are.

Truth exists before it is spoken of or described, and it is not changed by the fact that someone describes it poorly or well. It is there and is still known to God as it is. For this reason you can say in a very real way that God is Truth. One of the unmistakable signs that Jesus Christ recognized His own divine nature is that He also called Himself the Truth as well as the Way and the Life. Conceivably, if Christ had only called Himself the Way, His words might have been understood much as Buddhists understand those of their founder, who never identified himself as divine. But no one can misunderstand when Christ says, "I am the ... truth, and the life" (Jn 14:6). For this reason He can say, "You will know the truth, and the truth will make you free."

Not being philosophers, his hearers would have immediately thought that He was referring simply to descriptive truth. Truth, as it is, makes no compromises. It cuts no corners, adjusts to no one's opinion. Some truths are self-evident; others must be sought out. The truths of faith are mysterious and can only be partially known and must first be revealed.

What should our attitude be toward something as vast and mysterious as the truth? Not simple curiosity, not a compromising attitude. Our attitude toward ultimate truth, and truths derived from it, should be profound reverence and grateful acceptance. For Christians the truth comes from Sacred Scripture and then from the teaching of the Church. Christ said to His apostles, the foundation of His Church: "He who hears you hears me" (Lk 10:16).

I hear people say, "I don't think the Bible is right about that," or, "I don't believe this teaching." This shows an attitude of irreverence. It sees our own minds as the measure of everything. Would it not be better to say, What truth is the Bible communicating? What truth is the Church teaching? Once you learn to do this—search for the truth—you'll begin to realize what Jesus meant when He said, "You will know the truth, and the truth will make you free."

Prayer

Lord Jesus, you are the Truth. Send me Your Holy Spirit, that I may accept and grow in truth, that I may strive always to say what is true. At the end of my days may I come to You who are the Truth. Amen.

Thursday

Truly, truly, I say to you, if any one keeps my word, he will never see death.... Truly, truly, I say to you, before Abraham was, I am.

JOHN 8:51, 58

Perhaps this passage from St. John's Gospel, chapter 8, which should be read in its entirety, is the strongest statement of Christ's divinity in the readings before the Passion. We shall spend a longer time on it. A person familiar with Hebrew ways of speaking would know instantly why those who were listening to Jesus became so incensed. The name of God in Hebrew is understood to be "I am who am" (Ex 3:14). The word *Yahweh*, which represents this phrase in Hebrew, is never pronounced or even written on paper by devout Jews. How appalled His listeners must have been to hear this upstart preacher from the backwoods, this uneducated construction worker, clearly call Himself God! They were not prepared for expressions like this, even from the glorious Messiah that they looked for.

And so, on the one hand, we can understand their disdain and even their rage. They were religious people, and they spent a great deal of time and energy in being observant. Why were they so wrong, and why did Jesus castigate them in no uncertain terms? He calls them all liars (Jn 8:55). The answer is that they had great hardness of heart because they did not accept the signs He worked as incontrovertible evidence of His divinity. "But the testimony which I have is greater than that of John; for the works which the Father has granted me to accomplish, these very works which I am doing, bear me witness that the Father has sent me" (Jn 5:36).

We have mentioned that teachers or preachers, influenced by modern skepticism and trying to salvage the Christian faith in the face of such skepticism, describe these chapters of John's Gospel as some teaching of the early Church written decades later. In fact, they are tampering with the very foundation of the Church's belief in Christ in order to win over complete skeptics, who can never come over, since they lack the gift of faith.

No one can prove absolutely by purely rational arguments that Jesus of Nazareth either uttered or did not utter these words. No one who was accompanying Him at that time has been around for about nineteen hundred years. But there are two inescapable facts of history: One is that the Gospel of John comes down to us from the very early Church. It is the great mystical and spiritual document forming, more than any other single piece of writing, the Christian concept of Jesus and His self-knowledge.

The second fact, as we have stated, is that the Church has given the highest possible approval to the Scriptures as the inherent work of the Holy Spirit. While it is true that no one had a tape recorder when Christ spoke, the author of this Gospel must have taken his human responsibility very seriously. There is no doubt that what he wrote indicates that Jesus of Nazareth used His miracles to prove His divinity.

And He did this in a very practical, important way for His hearers. He linked faith in Him to life after death. In a dramatic way He indicated that the accepted notion of human death, the end of an individual's life, does not even apply to those who are true to His word. They will not see the same death that those who do not accept Him must experience.

Over the centuries the language of faith has been shaped by this belief. The Church teaches in the preface of the Mass for the Dead that "life is changed, not ended. When the body of our earthly dwelling lies in death, we gain an everlasting dwelling place in heaven."

Let your faith in the promise of salvation grow and grow. It can never grow too much. In the very dark years of spiritual trial that Mother Teresa records in her letters, she advises us to grow in our understanding of and participation in the redemption that Jesus has won for us. She wrote to the Missionaries of Charity:

> Try to increase your knowledge of the mystery of redemption. This knowledge will lead you to love, and love will make you share through your sacrifice in the passion of Christ. Jesus wanted to help us by sharing our life, our loneliness, our agony and death. All that He has taken upon Himself and has carried it in the darkest night. Only by being one with us has He redeemed us.... Pray thus when you find it hard: I wish to live in this world which is so far from God, which has turned so much from the light of Jesus, to help them [the poor]—to take upon myself something of their suffering.

In unbelieving times it is the most joyful of penances to bear witness to Christ and the salvation He won for us. This is called evangelization—the bringing of the Good News. Spend some time thinking about how you can know the Good News better. If you have never studied the new *Catechism of the Catholic Church* (1994; revised 1997) or the Church's teachings on salvation, carefully do so now. I wrote a very simple, readable book, *Healing the Original Wound* (Servant Publications, 1993), on this subject.

Unfortunately, many popular religious books at present do not focus on the mystery of salvation, thereby inadvertently reflecting the skepticism of our times. The fact is that you and I are going to die.

What will that death mean for us? Pray to be true to Christ's word so that you will never experience the death of those who do not believe, but rather that you will pass to eternal life.

Prayer

Lord Jesus, You alone are my Savior and the Savior of all whom I know and love. We cannot really know You without the grace of faith. Help us to grow in faith, and to be witnesses to faith. Help us to be thankful to be Your instruments to bring faith anew to the unbelieving world around us. Amen.

Friday

"If I am not doing the works of my Father, then do not believe me; but if I do them, even though you do not believe me, believe the works, that you may know and understand that the Father is in me and I am in the Father." ...

"John did no sign, but everything that John said about this man was true."

JOHN 10:37-38, 41

Jesus demands faith, and again we see that it must be based on the Father's works that He performs. His critics took Him very seriously and were going to stone Him (Jn 10:31). Jesus invoked the name and teaching of John the Baptist, whom many people took to be the "one who was sent" or at least a prophet. But John had called Jesus the Lamb of God, and these people were going to stone the One who is to take away the sins of the world.

Be careful that the Christ you believe in is not some pale caricature, a kind of nice man who was close to God, or even the greatest of all teachers about the way to God. He is not. He is the Lamb of God, the sacrifice that takes away the sins of the world. St. Paul, as well as the author of the Epistle to the Hebrews, sees Him as the sacrifice by which our sins are taken away and we are saved:

> For if many died through one man's trespass, much more have the grace of God and the free gift in the grace of that one man Jesus Christ abounded for many.... If, because of one man's trespass, death reigned through that one man, much more will those who receive the abundance of grace and the free gift of righteousness reign in life through the one man Jesus Christ. Then as one man's trespass led to condemnation for all men, so one man's act of righteousness leads to acquittal and life for all men. For as by one man's disobedience many were made sinners, so by one man's obedience many will be made righteous.
>
> ROMANS 5:15, 17-19

What can our response be? We have already spoken about evangelization, about spreading the Good News and bearing witness to Him in daily life. What about devotion to Him, prayers of thanksgiving, and sorrow for sin? What about the most powerful prayer of all—adoration?

This is the worship reserved to God alone. It is very different from devotion to any saint. It is an attempt at a complete prostration of ourselves before the Lord, an emptying out of everything else—not destruction, but a joyous offering.

Adoration is awesome when it is offered to God, to the mysterious Holy Trinity. Can we kneel in our imagination before the figure of a mortal man like ourselves—someone who could get tired and annoyed, who could be compassionate and who could argue? Can you adore a human being? That's what our Christian religion is about. Think of the apostles when Christ met them in the upper room after the Resurrection. They saw earth and heaven, time and eternity, man and God, all at once, and they worshipped Him: "My Lord and my God!" (Jn 20:28).

Take some time. Be quiet for a half an hour or so. Pull all your attention together, and see Him before the eyes of your mind on the roads of Galilee, on the Cross, or standing by the empty tomb. Pray in a way that you have never prayed before. Come, let us adore Him in silence.

Prayer

Jesus, I adore You in Your Person: God incarnate in the body and soul of a mortal man, one who can and does die. My Lord and my God. Amen.

Saturday

Many of the Jews therefore, who had come with Mary and had seen what he did, believed in him; but some of them went to the Pharisees and told them what Jesus had done. So the chief priests and the Pharisees gathered the council, and said, "What are we to do? For this man performs many signs. If we let him go on thus, every one will believe in him, and the Romans will come and destroy both our holy place and our nation." But one of them, Caiaphas, who was high priest that year, said to them, "You know nothing at all; you do not understand that it is expedient for you that one man should die for the people, and that the whole nation should not perish." He did not say this of his own accord, but being high priest that year he prophesied that Jesus should die for the nation, and not for the nation only, but to gather into one the children of God who are scattered abroad. So from that day on they took counsel how to put him to death.

JOHN 11:45-53

We have already seen how a proper understanding of the salvation won by Christ has been eroded in contemporary Christianity. It is a belief often left unpreached, poorly communicated in religious education, or perhaps not spoken of at all. Holy Week is a wonderful time to deepen your appreciation and gratitude to our Blessed Savior for the gift of salvation, of eternal life.

People often pass over this foundational belief of Christianity or understand it too narrowly, focusing only on themselves and their friends because there are so many mysteries surrounding redemption. They are just concerned about how they're going to be saved. In fact, many avoid this most significant belief because they feel that they cannot deal with what they cannot easily understand.

The incredible facts made clear in innumerable quotations in the New Testament are these: The world was fallen and all were lost. The Son of God took upon Himself a true human nature, body and soul, and endured what human life would bring Him without the protection of His divine power. Fully human as well as divine, He experienced our condition in every way except sin. And He did this to remove the universal condition of all human beings who were lost.

Satan entered into the hearts of men, who in their wickedness were responsible for His terrible death, which He always knew lay ahead of Him. He died in an act of obedience to God to endure the human situation and by His loving sacrifice to forgive and atone for all of the sins of the world. In the act of His sacrifice He forgives all who are responsible, all the sinners who lived or would live. He atoned for you and me. "And I, when I am lifted up from the earth, will draw all men to myself" (Jn 12:32).

But God shows His love for us in that while we were yet sinners Christ died for us. Since, therefore, we are now justified by His blood, much more shall we be saved by him from the wrath of God. For if while we were enemies we were reconciled to God by the death of his Son, much more, now that we are reconciled, shall we be saved by his life. Not only so, but we also rejoice in God through our Lord Jesus Christ, through whom we have now received our reconciliation.

ROMANS 5:8-11

It would be very helpful to memorize these quotations. Write them on your heart, so that when you are going through the events of Holy Week, you will think not only of what the Father and His Son have done for you but also of what you may do in return in adoration and in gratitude.

Prayer

The commemoration of Your death now comes, Lord Jesus. Help me this year by study, prayer, works of charity, and adoration to engrave on my mind and heart what it means to say that You are the Savior of the world. Amen.

Holy Week

Palm Sunday

*Most of the crowd spread their garments on the road, and others cut
branches from the trees and spread them on the road. And the crowds
that went before him and that followed him shouted, "Hosanna to
the Son of David! Blessed is he who comes in the name of the Lord!
Hosanna in the highest!"*

MATTHEW 21:8-9

This day commemorates the only real celebration of Jesus of
Nazareth as King and Messiah during His earthly life. Jewish
people celebrating the Passover at this time of the year still sing a joyous hymn to Elijah, with the chorus "Hosanna to the Son of David!
Blessed is he who comes in the name of the Lord!" It is obvious from
the hymn's context that it is not referring to the great prophet who
ascended to heaven in a fiery chariot but rather to the second Elijah,
the Promised One, the Messiah. For this reason some people thought
Jesus was Elijah (see Mt 16:14).

Because of His family lineage, Jesus was referred to as the Son of
David by the crowds on the first Palm Sunday. The believing Christian
rejoices today that the Son of God received this little recognition of

His divine vocation. Perhaps the procession into Jerusalem was the clearest possible acknowledgment of His messiahship since the homage paid Him by the wise men and the shepherds at the Nativity. How our own hearts can be thrilled at the words of the hymn "All Glory, Laud, and Honor to Thee, Redeemer King!" as we walk in solemn procession, which is now, sadly enough, often omitted "for practical considerations."

Processions were much more common in those times, the most solemn being the Royal Progress, as it was called, by the royalty. They rode in gilded carriages drawn by white stallions. There was no such procession for Jesus of Nazareth. This leads us to a more poignant lesson of Palm Sunday. Remember the little people whom Jesus loved and who were sarcastically referred to as the rabble on the occasion of the healing of the man born blind (see Jn 9)? It was these enthusiastic poor people, having nothing more elegant to offer the Messiah than a mule and branches torn from nearby trees, who celebrated Jesus' arrival. How sadly revealing this really is.

The poverty of this humble celebration did not pain Jesus, because He could have summoned legions of angels. No, it is sad for the human race. It was the best that men of the time could do and were willing to offer.

And we don't do much more right now. If you want to experience an enthusiastic reception for Jesus, go and pray with the poor, with the old black ladies in storefront churches, and with the Latinos in their soulful Holy Week processions. Every year the friars and sisters of our community walk with our friends through the debris-filled streets, giving out palms. The poor join in with joyous enthusiasm.

It is the best they can do. Apparently, the Son of God Himself knew that this humble crowd was the best He could find to proclaim that He was the Messiah, the new Elijah, the Son of David.

Religious practice in the English-speaking world has become very casual, to use a kindly term. "Slipshod" might be a better way to describe what we see going on. I am not simply referring to casual liturgical practice but even to the way people dress when coming to church and how they stand and kneel. Many of those who come to church do so in order to fulfill an obligation as painlessly as possible. There is no enthusiasm, joy, or engagement of the person. It seems to many that attending church is like getting on a bus.

We should work to change this slipshod approach. We should dress as if we were going to the worship of God and not to the beach. We should sing and respond to the prayers, and personally we should pray. When the liturgy is over, then we should joyfully greet our fellow Christians.

If all this seems strange and unreal, then go and pray with the poor. Like the crowd that welcomed Jesus, they will show you what to do.

Prayer

O Lord Jesus Christ, You come as our friend and also as our King. We look to You for consolation and understanding, and we should also look to You with adoration and thanksgiving. As this Holy Week begins, help us to realize that You are our suffering and crucified King, the poor little One, but nonetheless the One we shall worship at the end of our lives as King of kings and Lord of lords. Amen.

Monday

Mary took a pound of costly ointment of pure nard and anointed the feet of Jesus and wiped his feet with her hair; and the house was filled with the fragrance of the ointment.

JOHN 12:3

The Gospel chosen for this day dramatically opens a week of conflict characterized by a medieval poet as life and death drawn into a mysterious duel. In a few lines we find the dramatic and loving veneration of Mary, the treachery of Judas, and the ominous reference to the plans of the authorities to kill Jesus. The stage is being set for the drama of the ages, not a play but a reality that will forever affect the destiny of every human being.

The believing Christian will want to move through the history of the Passion in a most attentive way. This requires some work. Life goes on with its many distractions. If you are fortunate, you may get some time on Holy Thursday and a bit more on Good Friday. Holiday preparations may dominate Holy Saturday, although the celebration of the Easter Vigil may draw your attention back to the events that took place in Passion Week two millennia ago.

Today, at the beginning of the week, we should make a resolution not only to pay careful attention to the biblical accounts but also to live through these days as best we can by penance and prayer. The somber Gospel narrative summons each of us to focus our attention not only on the great events—the Last Supper, the Crucifixion, and Christ rising from the dead—but also on the details.

In the past, religious artists focused on each detail. On older altars we can still find symbols of the cock that crowed on Friday morning, the dice of the executioners who gambled for Jesus' clothes, and the nails of the Crucifixion. These objects, as well as every word spoken— from the words of Jesus to the cynical remarks of Pilate—all provide food for meditation.

Since the death of Christ more than one hundred thousand weeks have gone by, and all of them together have never had the significance of that Passion Week so long ago. Some have lived through Holy Week with the loving attention of John; others have been like some of the citizens of Jerusalem, wondering why the sun had become dark at noon.

Have you ever really tried to take the daily Scripture readings and the four Gospel accounts of the Passion as your guide through these events, which are the cornerstone of salvation history? We are invited to experience this week with a hauntingly beautiful Marian hymn, in which the Mother of Christ implores us:

> Oh, come and mourn with me awhile!
> See, Mary calls us to her side;
> Oh, come and let us mourn with her;
> Jesus, our Love, is crucified!

Prayer

O Lord Jesus Christ, give me the grace of the Holy Spirit to enter far more deeply than before into the mystery of salvation. Help me to do this by reading the Gospel accounts of Your Passion and death, by prayer and devout participation in the liturgy, and by fasting and genuine service to the poor and needy. Help me to make this a truly holy week. Amen.

Tuesday

Let not your hearts be troubled; believe in God, believe also in me. In my Father's house are many rooms; if it were not so, would I have told you that I go to prepare a place for you? And when I go and prepare a place for you, I will come again and will take you to myself, that where I am you may be also. And you know the way where I am going.

JOHN 14:1-4

I think this text is, from a personal point of view, the most important passage in the Bible. It speaks about the personal salvation that each of us must always be concerned about. We cannot honestly escape such a concern. It is the purpose of our very existence.

On the eve of the Passion, Christ clearly teaches His disciples and, through them, "all who will come to believe because of their teaching." Then He will come back and take us where He is going, to His Father's house. We have already considered this mystery of salvation and how we must not be preoccupied so exclusively with it that we see the whole worlds of nature and grace as focused on us and our eternal welfare. That could be a very neurotic and self-preoccupied form of piety. But not to include the promise of salvation in any serious consideration of the Christian life can be either pre-sumption (we are all going to heaven) or skepticism (eternity and personal salvation are just a big "perhaps").

St. John's Gospel brings this mystery clearly before us as we pre-pare to follow Jesus when He faces His death. From the viewpoint of the theologians it is most important that Jesus Christ clearly indi-cated that the purpose of His sacrifice was to win salvation for the nations and for all the individual children of God. We can never lose sight of this; yet the apostles, the other disciples, and those whom they would speak to in the coming hours would be deeply shaken by His death and completely unprepared for the Resurrection, which would come so quickly after it.

The providence of God and the wisdom of the Holy Spirit would give Jesus' words to countless numbers of faithful facing their own deaths or the death of someone dear to them. If you have been in dan-ger of death because of war, accident, or dangerous surgery, you may know how important these words are. "I go to prepare a place for you." When you have been standing by the bedside of someone very dear to you, with your heart broken and with the love you have cherished being taken from you, then you must have these other words on your lips and in your heart: "I will come again and will take you to myself."

Prayer

Lord Jesus, let Your words of victory over death be at the center of my life. May they never leave me. Otherwise, my life must be lived with denial or with the dullness of an animal or, worse, with total hopelessness. Help us to believe in You always, that You will take us to Your Father's house. Amen.

Wednesday

When Jesus had thus spoken, he was troubled in spirit, and testified, "Truly, truly, I say to you, one of you will betray me." The disciples looked at one another, uncertain of whom he spoke. One of his disciples, whom Jesus loved, was lying close to the breast of Jesus; so Simon Peter beckoned to him and said, "Tell us who it is of whom he speaks." So lying thus, close to the breast of Jesus, he said to him, "Lord, who is it?" Jesus answered, "It is he to whom I shall give this morsel when I have dipped it." So when he had dipped the morsel, he gave it to Judas, the son of Simon Iscariot. Then after the morsel, Satan entered into him. Jesus said to him, "What you are going to do, do quickly."

JOHN 13:21-27

In the past this day was usually called Spy Wednesday. The name put quite a chill into me as a boy, because it was wartime and we were constantly reminded by signs that there could be spies around. We even knew people who had had Nazi sympathies before the war, and although they had publicly given them up, you "never knew for sure."

Judas was the big spy. It was easy to hate him and to put him, as Dante had done, in the frozen fire at the bottom pit of hell. How could he ever betray Jesus? And with a kiss? And for money? It was the worst of all sins, and it was committed by an apostle.

We were also taught in those days that when we sinned we, too, betrayed Our Savior. It was and still is very frightening to think not only of the punishment our sins have earned us but also of our betrayal of the One who is so loving, so utterly unselfish in His willingness to suffer for me personally and for us all. If you have a personal devotion to Christ, then sin is not simply a violation of God's law, an act of disobedience and disorder against your Creator, a contradiction of the very reason for your existence, and even an affront to yourself. It is all of these things and much more.

With sin come the great guilt and sorrow of a friend betrayed, of a love abused, of selfishness that violates a faithful and generous affection. No truly devoted Christian can ever look on sin simply as a violation of the divine law. "If you love me, keep my commandments" (Jn 14:15). Judas did not stay to hear those words that night, but he surely knew that with Jesus, discipleship and obedience went together.

But he had betrayed his beloved Master. Why? Was he resentful that Christ did not establish the kind of kingdom the Jewish people expected with His divine powers and miracles? Was he disappointed with the humble Christ? Was he angry that he was not one of the three favorite apostles, Peter, James, and John? Was he just tired of the whole thing? There must have been reasons, and they were not thirty pieces of silver, which were only a month's pay of a day laborer.

Anyone wishing to be a disciple of Jesus must always keep in mind that Judas had his reasons; otherwise Satan could not have entered his heart. We who are trying to be devoted disciples commit sin. We sin by weakness, distraction, and, worse, omission caused by desire for human respect or negligence. We do not want to pay the price asked of us, or we fail to tell the truth. Although we may rarely or never directly betray Jesus as Judas did, we ought to be aware that we can. We could open our hearts to Satan out of disappointment, chagrin, or anger at Christ and His apparent weakness in the face of evil.

But the more likely possibility is that we will do what the other disciples did. We will not openly betray Him, but we will fail Him. We will fade out. We will not remain with Him.

Only a few went with Him into the utter darkness—several women and one man. That one man appears to have been His best friend. It was far more dangerous for him to stand by Jesus than it was for the women. The enemies of Jesus would perhaps have expected some women to walk alongside Him as He carried the Cross. It was a woman's thing to do in those days. But the beloved disciple went. One hundred years later St. Irenaeus was the first one to tell us that John is the author of this Gospel and the beloved disciple. This is plausible because the author calls himself an eyewitness.

I am not such a fool as to think that if I had been there, I would have been the faithful disciple. To be quite honest, I have to be constantly aware that I can and will fail Him in His hour of need. And that's enough to keep me very afraid and to be very grateful for His promise to Peter: "I have prayed for you that your faith may not fail; and when you have turned again, strengthen your brethren" (Lk 22:32). We need to watch and pray that we do not enter into temptation, that we do not betray Him.

Prayer

Lord Jesus, send Your Holy Spirit that we may not betray You. Send your comforting Spirit to strengthen us if we waver on the way. Enlighten our minds so that we can recognize a temptation to betrayal when it comes into our lives. Amen.

Holy Thursday

And when the hour came, he sat at table, and the apostles with him. And he said to them, "I have earnestly desired to eat this passover with you before I suffer; for I tell you I shall not eat it until it is fulfilled in the kingdom of God." And he took a cup, and when he had given thanks he said, "Take this, and divide it among yourselves; for I tell you that from now on I shall not drink of the fruit of the vine until the kingdom of God comes."

And he took bread, and when he had given thanks he broke it and gave it to them, saying, "This is my body which is given for you. Do this in remembrance of me." And likewise the cup after supper, saying, "This cup which is poured out for you is the new covenant in my blood."

LUKE 22:14-20

The Sacred Triduum—the three holy days (Thursday, Friday, and Saturday)—opens with joy and sorrow, love and betrayal, life and death, the promise of eternity and a feeling of impending death at the Last Supper. This is the great day of paradox—that is, apparent contradictions mysteriously containing truth. For example, we call this Passover meal the Last Supper. But these simple events are the beginning of billions of commemorations in Eucharistic liturgies. Could anyone there have imagined Bach's Mass in B minor, or a Mass performed by native Africans singing an accompaniment to the renewal of the Last Supper?

It's a very sorrowful meal. Christ promises the Eucharist, which has been the greatest single source of spiritual joy and consolation that the Christian world has ever known. Christ leaves the supper to be arrested; within eighteen terrible hours He will be tortured to death, and yet He tells us that He will be with us till the end of the world. The most significant sign of His presence is the bread and wine consecrated and transformed at the re-presentaton of this holy meal.

During the past several days we have been meditating on some of

His discourse to the apostles in John's Gospel. If you have been reading along, you realize that these pages, including John chapters 5 and 6 and chapters 13–17 (called the Book of Glory), contain the most profound revelation of who Jesus Christ is and what He can be to those who seek to love Him.

Try to take some time during the Holy Triduum to read and meditate on these events. Although they happened so long ago, they are repeated over and over till the end of the world.

Any thinking Christian knows that Christ is betrayed, abandoned, humiliated, and suffers hunger and thirst constantly in His members. "I was hungry and you gave me no food" (Mt 25:42). He is constantly on trial somewhere in the world, and He is left alone in our own neighborhoods in the sick and the dying.

The events of Holy Thursday are almost all incomplete realities. They look forward to what is to come for their completion. The very next day the Blood of the Eucharist must be shed and the Body must be broken. But even then, what do we see but the corpse of an atrociously abused man, like the image seen on the Shroud of Turin? We must keep going so that the Eucharist is not a funeral procession and the life of Christ is not just another noble failure. He lives! On the third day He comes back to life, never to die again. "I am with you always, to the close of the age" (Mt 28:20).

There is so much in the Last Supper, and then there is the agony in the garden and the arrest of Jesus. Start anywhere prayerfully and thoughtfully, and you will walk into the vast tunnels of a gold mine. The events of these days can teach us every year and, in fact, every day of every year, because they come back to us not only in our memories but also in the sacramental reality of the daily Eucharist.

Is there one word that can sum up Christ's deeds and our response as disciples? Obviously the word is love. It begins the account of the Last Supper in John 13:1: "Jesus knew that his hour had come to depart out of this world to the Father, having loved his own who were in the world, he loved them to the end."

The Gospel is above all a story of love, and love should be our response. St. Paul, who was called after all these things came to pass, summed it up so well in words that should guide our minds and hearts: "The charity of Christ urges us on" (2 Cor 5:14).

Prayer

Lord Jesus Christ, come and be with us throughout the days of our life, and remind us constantly of Your presence by the Holy Eucharist. May we live out in our own lives the events and the meaning of the Last Supper, and may we come at the end of our lives to that great banquet that began that night and that will last through all eternity. Amen.

Good Friday

And when they came to the place which is called The Skull, there they crucified him, and the criminals, one on the right and one on the left. And Jesus said, "Father, forgive them; for they know not what they do." And they cast lots to divide his garments. And the people stood by, watching; but the rulers scoffed at him, saying, "He saved others; let him save himself, if he is the Christ of God, his Chosen One!" The soldiers also mocked him, coming up and offering him vinegar, and saying, "If you are the King of the Jews, save yourself!" There was also an inscription over him, "This is the King of the Jews." One of the criminals who were hanged railed at him, saying, "Are you not the Christ? Save yourself and us!" But the other rebuked him, saying, "Do you not fear God, since you are under the same sentence of condemnation? And we indeed justly; for we are receiving the due reward of our deeds; but this man has done nothing wrong." And he said, "Jesus, remember me when you come in your kingly power." And he said to him, "Truly, I say to you, today you will be with me in Paradise."

LUKE 23:33-43

There are at least a thousand lessons to be learned at Calvary, and then there are the mysteries beyond these lessons, which bring us to the shores of an endless sea. But in keeping with our theme, the work of Christ as Savior and Redeemer, the forgiveness of sins by Christ on the Cross seems to be the lesson that we should concentrate on for these meditations.

Must it be said that we all need forgiveness? We need it for the offenses and failures we have visited on others, often those we love the most. When I speak to people who have dark and frightening sins from the past—a betrayal of love, an abortion, long years of living as a pagan far from God—sometimes they experience guilt over what was not seen even as a sin at the time and may not be now.

There are examples from wartime: the soldier who remembers shooting a boy who might have been carrying a bomb; the bombardier who pushed a button to release a shower of bombs over a city even though he knew his map had been falsified to indicate that his target was an ammunition depot. Then there is the evil we did not protest or contradict out of human respect or plain fatigue, or because we were preoccupied with our own needs. There are good works we did not stop to do because we were too busy or because we did not have the money at hand. Many times we failed to honor God, worshipped Him in an imperfect way, and showed a lack of gratitude to Christ, which may be dawning on us only now.

All these sins and failures were there at Calvary. I doubt that Jesus thought of them all, but then I can't know for sure, because He is a divine Person. Certainly I know that I made my contribution to the ocean of evil, the sins of the world that came down upon Him. When I ask myself how a God-man suffers, the answer comes back that He suffered as no other man—or all of us put together—can think or suffer.

And how did He act? The Gospel tells us that He could be very direct when pointing out hardness of heart, pride, arrogance, or a judgmental spirit. He could tell people off, and He does so in each of the Gospels. But once the Passion begins, He is very gentle and almost passive. For the most part He does not even respond to His enemies. He speaks to Pilate, giving him something to think about and leaving the rest of us with much to think about. But there are no reproaches, no condemnations, as there often were in the parables and in the other New Testament writers. In the words of St. Peter beginning in Acts 2:22, in the Epistles of James and John, one finds a holy reproach, a pointing out of sins, a call to repentance. Once Jesus was arrested—in fact, from the beginning of the Last Supper, with the exception of the mild reproach to Judas (a call to turn back perhaps)—there was no reproach. Jesus knew His hour had come, and He did not waste words or emotion in trying to stop the process. Pilate wondered at His silence (Mt 27:14).

What, then, is Jesus' attitude as all this terrible torture goes on? "As a sheep led to the slaughter or a lamb before its shearer is dumb, so he opens not his mouth" (Acts 8:32). St. Philip the apostle comments on this text from the prophecy of Isaiah (53:7) and explains to the eunuch that it refers to Jesus Christ. Most of us have never seen sheep going to be shorn or slaughtered, but they do not resist like other animals. It is a shocking image, but no more shocking than the silence, the prayer, the complete acceptance of the Messiah.

At the Yad Vashem Holocaust Museum in Jerusalem, I saw a horrible photograph of Jewish women—a grandmother, a mother, and two little girls—lined up to be shot in front of a trench already filled with the bodies of other women. I will never forget their looks of resignation and love as they grasped each other for the last time. As I looked into their eyes, I could see the look of Christ and His mother at the Cross.

The words of Jesus at the Cross speak of four things. The first is suffering: "I thirst." "My God, my God, why have you forsaken me?" (Lk 22:42). The second set of words is concerned with others, especially His mother—"Woman, this is your son"—and of the beloved disciple—"This is your mother."

He also speaks words of forgiveness and compassion for His enemies and, by a very reasonable extension, for all the world, which has sinned. "Father, forgive them; for they know not what they do." Then there is the promise of salvation to the poor thief, of which we will say something later.

There are words of trust as He calls on the Father: "Father, into your hands I commend my spirit" (Lk 23:4).

Except for the words "I thirst," to which many holy souls like Mother Teresa have given a spiritual significance ("I thirst for the love of souls"), all of Jesus' words are about others: the Father, His mother, the repentant thief, and all who have brought about His death. But there is no reproach, no condemnation, not even a warning, as there had been in Jerusalem on the Via Dolorosa (Lk 23:29-31). As Jesus comes to His hour, He trusts completely in God despite the terrible dark feelings of abandonment.

If you have never felt abandoned by God, do not even try to comprehend these words. If you have felt abandoned, then you can know what Jesus went through. Jesus went into the darkest of pits that the human mind can enter. When we remember that union with God was His whole being, His whole life from all eternity, then the fact that His humanity experienced abandonment by God is painful beyond anything we can imagine.

Jesus on the Cross is concerned with forgiveness. He pays no attention to the mockery; He hardly seems to relate to the terrible physical pain.

Medical experts claim He died of asphyxiation caused by a lack of oxygen, which in turn was caused by the loss of blood and a rupture of the esophagus from the way His body hung. I tend to doubt this, because such a death would have been preceded by a coma, however brief, from the shortage of oxygen. Surely His death had several causes, but He seems to have been quite conscious until the moment of death.

But He uses His time and His last energy to give a most important message: Sinners are forgiven. The thief who never walked on the straight way or entered by the narrow gate is forgiven. He who is the Son of God asks pardon for His killers—the scribes, the Pharisees, the high priest, Pilate, and the Romans.

Tradition tells us that the centurion who pierced His side and said, "Truly this man was the Son of God" (Mk 15:39) became a Christian and even an early priest. Tradition gives him the name St. Longinus. Whatever may have happened in the lives of these little people who were drawn into the drama of the ages, we know one thing for certain: Jesus forgave them all and asked pardon for them.

We must be as careful and accurate as possible in acknowledging our sins large and small, known acts and unknown omissions, deeds and attitudes, and bring them under the Cross as Jesus hangs on it. We must look at the incredible and mysterious event of the death of a God, the only God who ever died, and realize that it happened for us that we might live forever. We are forgiven—we need only accept and acknowledge the forgiveness and the need to repent, to change as much as we can.

We have two more things to do. As Jesus Christ made clear in His life and works: We also must forgive, and we must love and help others in return for what God has done for us.

Prayer

Jesus, I kneel beneath Your Cross. You are in glory, but here on earth You suffer and die every day in the poor, the sick, the abandoned, the abused, and the killed. Help me to recognize You and care for You, and give me the grace to forgive. Amen.

Holy Saturday

For Christ also died for sins once for all, the righteous for the unrighteous, that he might bring us to God, being put to death in the flesh but made alive in the spirit; in which he went and preached to the spirits in prison.

1 PETER 3:18–19

Something strange is happening—there is a great silence on earth today, a great silence and stillness. The whole earth keeps silence because the King is asleep. The earth trembled and is still because God has fallen asleep in the flesh and he has raised up all who have slept ever since the world began. God has died in the flesh, and hell trembles with fear.

He has gone to search for our first parent, as for a lost sheep. Greatly desiring to visit those who live in darkness and in the shadow of death, he has gone to free from sorrow the captives Adam and Eve, he who is both God and the son of Eve. The Lord approached them bearing the cross, the weapon that had won him the victory. At the sight of him Adam, the first man he had created, struck his breast in terror and cried out to everyone: "My Lord be with you all." Christ answered him: "And with your spirit." He took him by the hand and raised him up, saying: "Awake, O sleeper, and rise from the dead, and Christ will give you light."

From an ancient homily on Holy Saturday,
Liturgy of the Hours, II, 496-97

Holy Saturday is a day of mystery and fascination. We have said the words from the Creed thousands of times, "He descended into hell." This, in fact, is a poor translation. In Latin it reads, *"ad inferos,"* which does not mean hell (*inferno*) but rather the lower regions, that mysterious state of being where the souls of the dead awaited the salvation of the world. This is sometimes called the edge—in Latin, *limbo*, or the limit or verge.

The piety of the Middle Ages loved to speculate on this strange state of being. Many fascinating paintings of the time show Christ holding His triumphant banner in hand, throwing open the gates of the lower regions, and being welcomed by Adam and Eve. A touching modern rendition has St. Joseph speaking first, "Son, how is your mother?"

Being a person who loves mystery, which Einstein says is the cradle of science, art, and religion, I find Holy Saturday especially fascinating. It's a day to feed the poor and do good works, to get out the Easter food packages and lots of chocolate rabbits and pictures of the risen Christ for the very deprived children. And then there is the Vigil.

I know some people like to prolong the period of sorrow from Good Friday until the Vigil, and I respect that—the empty church, the open tabernacle, the sorrowful psalms. But let me enjoy my day of anticipation. I know what's going to happen. Of course, if I had been there in A.D. 33, I hope I'd be sitting with the completely distraught disciples, ashamed of our cowardly failure to be with Jesus in His hour. They were probably so distraught that they gave little thought to what, if anything, was going to happen next. But I can't reconstruct their sentiments that day as well as I can reconstruct Good Friday in my mind.

How sad life must be without a belief in the Resurrection. God must give special grace to those who do not know about it, just to keep them going. Why don't they take their own lives? I feel sorrier for the person who identifies himself as a Christian but for whom the Resurrection of Christ is only a symbol or a myth or some other nonsense.

Life has lots of sorrows, lots of Via Dolorosas, and if you live long enough, several trips to Calvary. But it only has one Easter. Let's get ready.

Prayer

Lord Jesus, long ago You called our ancestors out of the lower regions. You led captivity captive. Send Your Holy Spirit to fill my heart with Easter hope and joy on this day when You were gone, only to return. Amen.

Easter Week

Easter Sunday

Now on the first day of the week Mary Magdalene came to the tomb early, while it was still dark, and saw that the stone had been taken away from the tomb. So she ran, and went to Simon Peter and the other disciple, the one whom Jesus loved, and said to them, "They have taken the Lord out of the tomb, and we do not know where they have laid him." Peter then came out with the other disciple, and they went toward the tomb. They both ran, but the other disciple outran Peter and reached the tomb first; and stooping to look in, he saw the linen cloths lying there, but he did not go in. Then Simon Peter came, following him, and went into the tomb; he saw the linen cloths lying, and the napkin, which had been on his head, not lying with the linen cloths but rolled up in a place by itself. Then the other disciple, who reached the tomb first, also went in, and he saw and believed; for as yet they did not know the scripture, that he must rise from the dead.

JOHN 20:1-9

We are so familiar with the accounts of the Resurrection that it is difficult for us to capture any sense of the total astonishment of the first witnesses. To begin with, there are no adequate words to describe what had never occurred before to human beings. Again we are plunged into the deepest mystery. We can understand the words, but we cannot totally fathom their inner meaning.

Perhaps it may give some sense of the mystery to say that for the first time since the material creation began (and that is mystery enough, as is even the word *matter*), there is a complex living organism, a human body and mind, that will never end and never know death again. Time and eternity, both mysterious, have come together in a thing of time, a living human body, which will never perish or cease living or even cease breathing. This must be at least part of His meaning when Jesus of Nazareth says, "I am the life."

This, of course, did not dawn on Mary or the apostles when they encountered the risen Christ. They must have thought, "He is dead, and somehow He is alive, and it is really He. He still has His wounds."

That it happened is a matter of faith. You must believe, and faith like this is a gift from God similar to hope and love. In the biblical sense they go beyond the limits of human moral virtue or natural good qualities. These three theological virtues are impossible to unaided human nature.

Those who decide to penetrate the impenetrable and fathom the unfathomable all come up with explanations that ultimately only inspire skepticism.

"He came back spiritually from the dead," some say. So, apparently, does Elvis Presley.

Others say, "He would not be remembered if He had not come back in some way." That's a bit of an improvement, but Gautama

Buddha has Him beat. He is remembered after three thousand years.

What about the faith of billions of people through two millennia who have believed that He rose from the dead? That's a better argument and should make us listen at least to what Christianity has to say.

But to use the words of Cardinal Newman, you have to bend your stiff neck to decide that your mind is not the measure of all things in heaven and on earth. You have to accept the words of the prophets and the apostles who have seen and heard the sights and sounds of eternity. You have to receive the kingdom of God like a little child or you cannot enter it, Christ himself tells us (Lk 18:17).

The restoration of the ancient Easter Vigil is filled with rich liturgical symbolism. It can make your heart and mind sing together, "Christ is risen." If it is celebrated with the poor, it pulses with their simple faith, which is so great that Christ seems almost visible. In the Eastern Church the people powerfully shout out, "He is risen, He is truly risen."

But even the liturgy is not essential. Even if sickness, distance, persecution, or imprisonment prevents us from celebrating the Eucharist, which so powerfully lets us know that Christ is risen, we can grasp this faith in the depth of the soul and grow in it by constant affirmation that Christ is risen. And He is risen not only on Easter but He is risen forever.

There was a day in my life when Easter frightened me. It was a dark, lonely, dreary time of suffering and oppression, all the more discouraging because the oppressors were good people caught in an outmoded system. I loved Good Friday and I still do. I've seen many people on the Cross, and I've been there myself a few times, but I've never seen anyone risen from the dead. That's where faith comes in. Good Friday is the day of the suffering God, the God of love. Easter is the Resurrection, the day of the God of faith. It is a day to recover from the effects of little faith, watered-down faith, lukewarm faith. It is the day to believe—that is, to assent with all your mind and heart and strength to the mystery that God has revealed and to realize that this assent gives life its only real sense.

The Bible lets us know that by faith all truly great things were accomplished in human history.

By faith Abraham obeyed when he was called to go out to a place which he was to receive as an inheritance; and he went out, not knowing where he was to go. By faith he sojourned in the land of promise, as in a foreign land, living in tents with Isaac and Jacob, heirs with him of the same promise. For he looked forward to the city which has foundations, whose builder and maker is God. By faith Sarah herself received power to conceive, even when she was past the age, since she considered him faithful who had promised. Therefore from one man, and him as good as dead, were born descendants as many as the stars of heaven and as the innumerable grains of sand by the seashore....

By faith Abraham, when he was tested, offered up Isaac, and he who had received the promises was ready to offer up his only son, of whom it was said, "Through Isaac shall your descendants be named." He considered that God was able to raise men even from the dead; hence he did receive him back and this was a symbol. By faith Isaac invoked future blessings on Jacob and Esau. By faith Jacob, when dying, blessed each of the sons of Joseph, bowing in worship over the head of his staff. By faith Joseph, at the end of his life, made mention of the exodus of the Israelites and gave directions concerning his burial.

By faith Moses, when he was born, was hid for three months by his parents, because they saw that the child was beautiful; and they were not afraid of the king's edict. By faith Moses, when he was grown up, refused to be called the son of Pharaoh's daughter, choosing rather to share ill-treatment with the people of God than to enjoy the fleeting pleasures of sin. He considered abuse suffered for the Christ greater wealth than the treasures of Egypt, for he looked to the reward. By faith he left Egypt, not being afraid of the anger of the king; for he endured as seeing him who is invisible. By faith he kept the Passover and sprinkled the blood, so that the Destroyer of the first-born might not touch them.

By faith the people crossed the Red Sea as if on dry land; but the Egyptians, when they attempted to do the same, were drowned. By faith the walls of Jericho fell down after they had been encircled for seven days....

And all these, though well attested by their faith, did not receive what was promised, since God had foreseen something better for us, that apart from us they should not be made perfect.

Therefore, since we are surrounded by so great a cloud of witnesses, let us also lay aside every weight, and sin which clings so closely, and let us run with perseverance the race that is set before us, looking to Jesus the pioneer and perfecter of our faith, who for the joy that was set before him endured the cross, despising the shame, and is seated at the right hand of the throne of God.

HEBREWS 11:8-12; 17-30; 39-12:2

Take your time today. Pray and give thanks and adore the risen Christ, alive with His divinity but above all in His humanity, in His Body and Blood in the Eucharist, alive in the eyes of charity in all who suffer. Say it over and over to yourself. Christ is risen. He is truly risen.

Prayer

O risen Lord Jesus, You will be as real to me as I let You be. Give me Your Holy Spirit to increase my faith, and deliver me from the fear of believing beyond my strength so that I may respond to You in faith. Let me help others to rejoice that You are truly risen from the dead. Amen.

Easter Monday

Now after the sabbath, toward the dawn of the first day of the week, Mary Magdalene and the other Mary went to see the sepulchre. And behold, there was a great earthquake; for an angel of the Lord descended from heaven and came and rolled back the stone, and sat upon it. His appearance was like lightning, and his raiment white as snow. And for fear of him the guards trembled and became like dead men. But the angel said to the women, "Do not be afraid; for I know that you seek Jesus who was crucified. He is not here; for he has risen, as he said. Come, see the place where he lay. Then go quickly and tell his disciples that he has risen from the dead, and behold, he is going before you to Galilee; there you will see him. Lo, I have told you." So they departed quickly from the tomb with fear and great joy, and ran to tell his disciples. And behold, Jesus met them and said, "Hail!" And they came up and took hold of his feet and worshiped him. Then Jesus said to them, "Do not be afraid; go and tell my brethren to go to Galilee, and there they will see me."

MATTHEW 28:1-10

Here we are rejoicing in the faith of the risen Christ and we run into a problem. The account in Matthew is quite different—much more dramatic than the one in John, closer to Mark and Luke, but somewhat different in each case. Much speculation and strongly different opinions exist over which account is the oldest and which account comes closest to the actual historical events. The great discrepancy may be the words of Jesus that the disciples will see Him in Galilee, and yet in Mark and Luke He sees the apostles together in Jerusalem.

The first thing we learn from this is that those who claim that each word of the Bible is literally, historically true, each standing by itself (the group that likes biblical one-liners), cannot be accurate. Reading these accounts one after another should make that fairly clear. But we are still left with the question about which account is most accurate in the historical sense. What actually happened?

This is a case in which no answer is the best answer, because it teaches us the most. Modern Catholic scholars, because they are believers, have the opinion that John's rather sober account is the closest to what happened, but they tend to drop out the angels, saying that they were added for effect. I repeat that these scholars were not there. There is absolutely no scientific way to say which human beings were there or not, much less the angels.

One account may fit in better with our way of thinking, but who is to say that our way of thinking in the twentieth century is going to last? By the year 3000, we may all be closer to cavemen. Our way of thinking changed a great deal in the twentieth century and took several unexpected detours. Are we going to think the same way about the Resurrection in the future?

The inescapable fact is that there are four accounts given by the providence of God and under the inspiration of the Holy Spirit. The word of God is the truth on which believers must unanimously agree and which they must know. That word tells us that Jesus Christ, having been crucified and having risen from the dead, appeared as a living man with His wounds to a large number of people over a period of several weeks. He was the same person the people had known before His death; He had flesh and bones and wounds; He was dead and now He lives.

Rather than preferring one account to another, why not learn from each of them? Matthew proclaims a cosmic event. His account reminds us of the astrophysicist's attempt to describe the first moments of the existence of the cosmos. Since I was not there, I read Matthew with reverence and awe, and I speculate about these events that must have really happened with a certain amount of humor. What did Caiaphas say when he first got the news? What did Mrs. Pilate say to the political hack she was married to? What did Peter's mother-in-law say up in Capernaum?

I think I know what she said. I heard the words from the little old ladies in Harlem when I walked through the grieving streets that dreadful spring evening in 1968, after the death of Martin Luther King Jr. They were standing around on the streets filled with people in their black coats and funeral hats, crying and holding their Bibles and saying, "Our King will never die." It was Matthew's account that opened my mind to what the Resurrection of Jesus meant to these people who knew their Bible so well.

Prayer

Holy Spirit, strengthen our faith and lift up our hearts so that we may
be filled with the same awe as those who saw the angel of the Lord
come down. Amen.

Tuesday

But Mary stood weeping outside the tomb, and as she wept she
stooped to look into the tomb; and she saw two angels in white,
sitting where the body of Jesus had lain.... They said to her,
"Woman, why are you weeping?" She said to them, "Because
they have taken away my Lord, and I do not know where they
have laid him." Saying this, she turned round and saw Jesus
standing, but she did not know that it was Jesus. Jesus said to
her, "Woman, why are you weeping? Whom do you seek?"
Supposing him to be the gardener, she said to him, "Sir, if you
have carried him away, tell me where you have laid him, and I
will take him away." Jesus said to her, "Mary." She turned and
said to him in Hebrew, "Rabboni!" (which means Teacher).
Jesus said to her, "Do not hold me, for I have not yet ascended
to the Father; but go to my brethren and say to them, I am
ascending to my Father and your Father, to my God and your
God." Mary Magdalene went and said to the disciples, "I have
seen the Lord."

JOHN 20:11-18

I have to confess that this is my favorite Resurrection account, but not because I think it is more realistic than others. Who cares what I think or what anyone else thinks about realism from our limited perspective? I like this account because poor hysterical Mary—the woman with the alabaster jar of ointment who washed Jesus' feet—may be the same woman Christ delivered from seven devils. She is the first witness in this account. Having worked with the Mary Magdalenes of the world, I would be delighted to learn, on arriving in eternity, that they give us such information (it may no longer be rel-evant) that John's Gospel had the historical story straight. In the meantime I can hope. Even though I wasn't there, I could speculate that this is the most plausible historical account.

You may think my reason a bit odd. Converted sinners, who are often a bit histrionic, colorful, and even missing a few chips for a full computer, are the most intriguing religious people around. If they are Catholic, they practically live in church. I've seen them even in Orthodox churches in Greece and the Near East. If they are Protestant, they read the Bible by the hour and love to go to prayer meetings.

My argument that Mary Magdalene was the first witness to the Resurrection is based on a psychological evaluation for her behavior. Mary was one of those souls who go to everything. If you lived in Jerusalem at that time and went to everything, you would have been at the Resurrection, too. Some of you may be bothered and annoyed and in various ways turned off by the Mary Magdalenes of this world. Ask yourself how you would appreciate this woman who is so involved with her crying that at first she fails to recognize who she is speaking to. The risen Christ has to calm her down, telling her, "Do not hold me."

I would never want to be accused of biblical speculation, and Scripture scholars can't stand psychologists, but Mary is not hard to diagnose. Why was she the first one there, and why in God's providence do we have this almost humorous account of a most solemn event? Why would Christ choose Mary? Maybe after His Resurrection He continued to have the same preference for little people and poor sinners that He showed in the earlier parts of the Gospel.

The next time offbeat people get on your nerves, remember this mysterious early morning scene. The little people had their day that first Easter morn.

Prayer

Lord Jesus, help me to appreciate the little people, the flaky people, the driven, and the naïve. I don't know what battles they have fought or what devils they have been delivered from. Help me to keep in mind the scene in the early morning outside Jerusalem and that Your Holy Spirit gave us this account of Your Resurrection. Amen.

Wednesday

That very day two of them were going to a village named Emmaus ... and talking with each other about all these things that had happened. While they were talking and discussing together, Jesus himself drew near and went with them. But their eyes were kept from recognizing him. And he said to them, "What is this conversation which you are holding with each other as you walk?" ... One of them, named Cleopas, answered him, "Are you the only visitor to Jerusalem who does not know the things that have happened there in these days?" And he said to them, "What things?" And they said to him, "Concerning Jesus of Nazareth, who was a prophet mighty in deed and word before God and all the people, and how our chief priests and rulers delivered him up to be condemned to death, and crucified him. But we had hoped that he was the one to redeem Israel.... Moreover, some women of our company ... were at the tomb early in the morning and did not find his body; and they came back saying that they had even seen a vision of angels, who said that he was alive...." And he said to them, "O foolish men, and slow of heart to believe all that the prophets have spoken! Was it not necessary that the Christ should suffer these things and enter into his glory?" And beginning with Moses and the prophets, he interpreted to them in all the scriptures the things concerning himself.

So they drew near to the village to which they were going... [and] he went in to stay with them. When he was at table with them, he took the bread and blessed, and broke it, and gave it to them. And their eyes were opened and they recognized him; and he vanished out of their sight. They said to each other, "Did not our hearts burn within us while he talked to us on the road, while he opened to us the scriptures?" And they rose that same hour and returned to Jerusalem; and they found the eleven gathered together and those who were with them, who said, "The Lord has risen indeed, and has appeared to Simon!" Then they told what had happened on the road, and how he was known to them in the breaking of the bread.

LUKE 24:13-35

Some Scripture scholars think that this wonderful account of the two disciples on the road to Emmaus is fictitious because it is filled with such realistic details. You can't win. The only thing I know for sure from such observations is that some people are jaded by skepticism. Pray for them.

To repeat the familiar refrain in this book, the Holy Spirit gave us this account, and from it we must learn several important things. The account of the disciples' journey to Emmaus is so realistic that most of us have enough imagination to put ourselves in the picture. I know I never would have made it to Calvary, but I might have made it to Emmaus.

Now, what do we learn? The prophets had taught that it was necessary for the Messiah to suffer these things in order to enter His glory. And then "beginning with Moses and all the prophets, he interpreted to them in all the scriptures the things concerning him-self." I wish the disciples had kept notes.

I got a phone call one day from an intelligent laywoman who was taking a course on the Gospel offered by a diocese and taught by reli-gious. The students were being taught that none of the Old Testament prophecies referred to Jesus. When I asked what they referred to, she said they did not refer to anything in the New Testament, meaning nothing that was in the future at the time of the prophets.

What do you call this? Skepticism? No. I call it an outrageous denial of the whole Christian tradition of biblical scholarship. And I call it humbug to boot. It reminds me of some European scholars who a century ago claimed rather stupidly that the prophecy of Isaiah had really been written after the death of Jesus and that is why it appeared to foretell the events of Jesus' life and death. Needless to say, Jewish scholars of the time were not amused. Many people were later amused, however, when the Dead Sea Scrolls were found to contain a copy of Isaiah, carbon-dated from before the time of Christ. They were prophecies.

Whenever I hear that the Jewish Scriptures, which we call the Old Testament, do not tell us about Christ, I recall that God's Providence has given us this account in which the Messiah Himself applies the Scriptures to His own life and death.

Like many religious people, I love oratorios. This genre of music was designed, as the name indicates, for a prayer group (the word deriving ultimately from the Latin *orare*, to pray, or *oratio*, prayer). After the Genovese lay reformer and saint Catherine Adorno started the Oratory of Divine Love at the end of the fifteenth century, this form of music was developed. It consisted of biblical passages, hymns, and prayers. The best-known of these oratorios is Handel's *Messiah*, but there are many others beginning with the original Italian works of Palestrina. If you don't have a recording of *The Messiah*, get it and listen to the Easter sections and then to the whole work. When Handel composed the work, in twenty-one days, he said he did not know whether he was "in the body or out of the body" (see 2 Cor 12:2). He hardly ate or slept during the work, and he wrote so quickly that the pages of the manuscript stuck to one another because the ink did not have a chance to dry. He wove the Old and New Testaments together with hymns in a beautiful way.

Now, can I ask you a question as a psychologist? How did the two men feel when they knew Him at the breaking of the bread? How did they feel running all the way back to Jerusalem? How did all the apostles feel when the two appeared at the door? Those who had been to Emmaus must have thought that no one would believe their story, but then they received the word that Christ had appeared to Simon. I get goose bumps thinking of that scene.

When *The Messiah* is sung—and it is a great event—and the marvelous Hallelujah chorus comes along, the audience usually stands. This custom goes back to King George II, who spontaneously stood when he first heard it sung. But there are always a few people in the concert hall who do not stand. They remind me of the skeptics, even the skeptical Christians. What is their response to the fact that the Emmaus account is given to us by the Holy Spirit to guide us on our way to salvation? Maybe they would be too bored to answer.

Prayer

Lord Jesus, let me know You along the road and in the Scriptures and especially in the breaking of the bread. And please send Your Spirit to those who do not realize that Moses and the prophets said You must suffer these things and so enter Your glory. Amen.

Thursday

As they were saying this, Jesus himself stood among them, and said to them, "Peace to you." But they were startled and frightened, and supposed that they saw a spirit. And he said to them, "Why are you troubled, and why do questionings rise in your hearts? See my hands and my feet, that it is I myself; handle me, and see; for a spirit has not flesh and bones as you see that I have." And when he had said this, he showed them his hands and his feet. And while they still disbelieved for joy, and wondered, he said to them, "Have you anything here to eat?" They gave him a piece of broiled fish, and he took it and ate before them.

Then he said to them, "These are my words which I spoke to you, while I was still with you, that everything written about me in the law of Moses and the prophets and the psalms must be fulfilled." Then he opened their minds to understand the scriptures, and said to them, "Thus it is written, that the Christ should suffer and on the third day rise from the dead, and that repentance and forgiveness of sins should be preached in his name to all nations, beginning from Jerusalem. You are wit-nesses of these things."

LUKE 24:36-48

If you did not meditate on yesterday's reading from St. Luke's Gospel, please read it before you begin this meditation. This account of the meeting of the risen Lord with the frightened disciples is filled with realism. It makes very clear that they did not see an apparition or what they thought was a ghost; they saw a living man. Finally, as their fear turned into amazed joy, it must have been a joy beyond words.

Our Lord ate a piece of fish, proving that He was not just a spirit. Here's a nice mystery for you: Does an everlasting body eat? Well, heaven is compared to a feast several times in Scripture. I have not been there, but I am intrigued by the idea.

After proving to the disciples that He had a real human body, although indeed changed, Our Lord again returns to the Scriptures, but this time the psalms are included among those writings that refer to Him. He teaches that His Passion and Resurrection were foretold in the prophets, and then He gives them their lifework to do. He had of course told them their mission before, that they were to preach repentance and forgiveness of sins to all nations. But this commission is something new in a way. During His earthly life He had insisted that He was sent to "the lost sheep of the house of Israel." Now He speaks of all nations.

Whatever your vocation or place in life, you are called to preach repentance and the forgiveness of sins if you wish to be Christ's follower. Look for opportunities to do this in ways that are suited to the needs of others. St. Paul gives us practical wisdom when he tells us: "Conduct yourselves wisely toward outsiders, making the most of the time. Let your speech always be gracious, seasoned with salt, so that you may know how you ought to answer every one" (Col 4:5-6).

If your life is such that you cannot realistically preach the message of forgiveness even by example, then pray the Lord of the harvest to send laborers into His harvest (see Lk 10:2). Christ said that the fields were white and ready for the harvest. They certainly are ripe as we begin the third millennium. And Jesus Christ asks this of you, as if you were standing among the disciples in that room the night of this mysterious and joyous scene.

Prayer

Lord Jesus, make me Your disciple. Help me to be a witness in my own place. Inspire me to pray often to the Lord of the harvest and to go into the harvest fields wherever I am. Amen.

Friday

Jesus said to them, "Come and have breakfast." Now none of
the disciples dared ask him, "Who are you?" They knew it was
the Lord. Jesus came and took the bread and gave it to them,
and so with the fish. This was now the third time that Jesus
was revealed to the disciples after he was raised from the dead.

JOHN 21:12-14

I once walked along the beach by the Sea of Galilee near Capernaum
in the early hours of the morning, with the mist rising through the
dawn. I felt it was important to feel the wet air on my face and the
ground underfoot so that the reality of the risen Christ would be all
the more clear to me. And it was.

When we read about these mysterious events, which can seem
almost like legends, symbols, or even dramas, we must remember
that they are the words of witnesses. These words resemble in some
way the style of Luke's Gospel. But they also bear the marks of John's
style. What is certain is that they are in all known copies of the
Gospel of St. John. If they are all the words of God, what difference
does it really make?

To be in the Holy Land, to walk the lanes of old Nazareth, to
shuffle along with the crowds on the Via Dolorosa, to climb the steps
to the house of Caiaphas—all these experiences make the Scriptures
more vivid and give them a geographic and historical point of reference in our lives. It may be a long time before pilgrims can go again
to the Holy Land, but if you ever can, do it. And try to walk in the

morning mist by the little harbor adjacent to the ruins of Capernaum on the Sea of Galilee, which is also referred to in Scripture as the Sea of Tiberias and the Lake of Gennesaret.

The Gospel puts in the incredibly human detail that Christ gave them a fish breakfast. Why the fire, the fish, and the bread? To let you and me know again that He was not an apparition but rather the same Jesus of Nazareth they had known, and He was humanly concerned about their needs even in His risen state. How awesome and great is the God of revelation, and yet how capable of little acts and humble deeds—a God who serves breakfast. "I am among you as one who serves" (Lk 22:27).

This is only the beginning. For the past two thousand years Christ has been with His followers in innumerable ways and circumstances. It may be in the silent mystery of Holy Communion or in a prayer said at the bedside of a dying friend. It may be at an event of lifelong significance—a marriage or an ordination—or merely at breakfast. He is with us. "It is the Lord." Let genuine prayer teach you this, and you will not even have to ask, "Who are You?" You will know.

Prayer

Lord Jesus, make Your presence known to me and to all I care about, to all in need or in trouble. Come to us in the little things of life, and let us know that You are with us, even at breakfast. Most of all, give us Your Holy Spirit always, that we will know that You rose from the dead and that we will, too. Amen.

Saturday

Afterward he appeared to the eleven themselves as they sat at table; and he upbraided them for their unbelief and hardness of heart, because they had not believed those who saw him after he had risen. And he said to them, "Go into all the world and preach the gospel to the whole creation."

MARK 16:14-15

The Gospel of Mark with its usual brevity and cryptic style sums up these days after the Resurrection. The evangelist describes the events that permitted the apostles and disciples to cope with the mysterious reality that surrounded them. It was a time to be astonished, to rejoice, to overcome doubts. But now their work must begin. They must go into the whole world and bring the good news of Christ.

Our Lord's words at this time did not refer to the four Gospels, which were not written for some time. The original Gospel (or good news) is a summary of the facts of Christ's life and the purpose of His human existence—redemption and salvation.

If you have followed these meditations and read the Scriptures they are based on, as well as the accounts of the Passion and Resurrection, your head may be spinning a bit. Mystery upon mystery, wonder upon wonder—all breaking through the superficial organization of everyday events that we call life. By prayer, meditation, and loving deeds, these daily events may gradually be transformed. Even sorrow and spiritual trial, sickness and old age, may begin to glow, though at first faintly, with the inner light of the Resurrection. The Holy Spirit must guide and strengthen you and lift you up in a way. But if you let it happen, your life will be suffused with the light of the first Easter and Pentecost.

An interesting example may be taken from art. In the nineteenth century a large number of painters portrayed the material world glowing with an inner light. Some belonged to the Hudson River School, but the movement spread throughout the Western world, with paintings of volcanoes in South America, the ruins of ancient Greece and Rome, even the ice fields of the Far North. Names like Frederic Church, Albert Bierstadt, and so many others filled gallery after gallery with scenes of mountains and valleys, rivers and lakes, all of which shone with a mystical light. It is quite an accomplishment to use the exclusively natural to evoke a profound sense of the supernatural. Whenever I see these paintings, they are a deep religious experience for me.

I think that this is what the disciples of Christ also see in every generation. They make their way through this world, but in the most commonplace things they encounter a transfiguring light and, with it, a presence. It is not a cosmic god, a metaphysical spirit, a poetic muse. It is what the apostles saw in the mountains of Galilee and by the lake. It is a human and divine presence, a Person who says, "Do not be afraid; it is I."

Prayer

Lord Jesus, risen Savior, please always make Your presence known, even in the darkest moments, even in the greatest distraction. Be with us, and we shall live. Amen.

Second Sunday of Easter

Divine Mercy Sunday

Jesus said to them again, "Peace be with you. As the Father has sent me, even so I send you." And when he had said this, he breathed on them, and said to them, "Receive the Holy Spirit. If you forgive the sins of any, they are forgiven; if you retain the sins of any, they are retained."

JOHN 20:21-23

The week after Easter and the following Sunday have occasionally been called the time of Divine Mercy. Our Lord had risen from the dead, and He met many people who had failed Him badly. The apostles and the disciples had run away and left Him. Except for His Mother, the holy women, and John, He had gone to the Cross alone. He came back from the dead, and He was merciful and kind to those who had failed Him.

A few years ago this Sunday was designated by Pope John Paul II as Divine Mercy Sunday. It was on this Sunday (in 2000) that the Pope canonized St. Faustina Kowalska, the apostle of Divine Mercy, the first saint of the new millennium. The private revelations given to this humble young Polish nun have mesmerized countless numbers of Catholics and even other Christians toward the end of the twentieth century. They were carefully studied for ten years by a theologian under the direction of Pope John Paul II when he was Archbishop of Krakow.

The message of Divine Mercy is most consoling in the difficult times in which we live. The conversation of Christ, the Divine Mercy, with the lost soul in the revelations of St. Faustina has given great hope to those whose relatives and friends left this life apparently unprepared. St. Faustina wrote that Christ had revealed to her that He calls all souls at the moment of death and offers them the grace of conversion. They are free, of course, to reject it or receive it.

This revelation, which may seem startling, is completely consistent with the salvation of the good thief on the cross, a man who apparently had not led a good life in any way. It also reminds us of Christ's prayer on the Cross, "Father, forgive them; for they know not what they do" (Lk 23:34).

As Lent and Easter pass into our memories, we face the coming months with the beautiful image of Divine Mercy—really an alternate image of the Sacred Heart of Jesus, according to St. Faustina. The loving heart of Our Savior calls us all individually to come to Him for forgiveness, healing, and salvation. As these meditations end, how beautiful it is that they end on the theme of Divine Mercy.

Prayer

O Lord Jesus Christ, the Mercy of God, You descended into this world to reveal the Father to us in ways that no one else ever did or ever could. Your message of mercy is an immense consolation to those struggling to practice their faith who have dear ones and friends who have been enticed by the spirit of the world. We are renewed in our prayers for them by the hope of Divine Mercy.

We pray for our world, which appears to be in such desperate need of divine forgiveness. This new century has begun with acts of violence and terrorism, but behind all of the dreadful pictures and scenes is a face that is calm, peaceful, and loving, calling to us. You say to us in that image, "Come to Me." And we say in response, "Jesus, I trust in You." Amen.

Hymns

The following hymns are suitable for meditation or singing during the holy seasons of Lent and Easter. They should help us to be compassionate with our suffering Savior and joyful with our victorious King.

Oh, Come and Mourn With Me Awhile!

Oh, come and mourn with me awhile!
See, Mary calls us to her side;
Oh, come and let us mourn with her;
Jesus, our Love, is crucified!

Have we no tears to shed for Him,
While soldiers scoff and Jews deride?
Ah! look how patiently He hangs;
Jesus, our Love, is crucified!

How fast His hands and feet are nailed;
His blessed tongue with thirst is tied;
His failing eyes are blind with blood;
Jesus, our Love, is crucified!

Seven times He spoke, seven words of love,
And all three hours His silence cried
For mercy on the souls of men;
Jesus, our Love, is crucified!

Death came, and Jesus meekly bowed;
His failing eyes He strove to guide
With mindful love to Mary's face,
Jesus, our Love, is crucified!

Come take thy stand beneath the Cross
And let the blood from out that Side
Fall gently on thee, drop by drop,
Jesus, our Love, is crucified!

—Frederick Faber

Frederick W. Faber (1814-63), who took Anglican orders in 1837 and was part of the Oxford Movement, was received into the Catholic Church in 1845. He was immensely successful as a preacher, and his books (for example, *All for Jesus, The Foot of the Cross, Bethlehem*) were popular for generations after his death. The author of nearly one hundred hymns, Fr. Faber founded the London Oratory in 1849.

The Regal Dark Mysterious Cross

The regal dark mysterious cross
In song is lifted high,
The wood on which our God was raised
As Man against the sky.

Upon this wood his body bore
The nails, the taunts, the spear,
Till water flowed with blood to wash
The whole world free of fear.

At last the song that David sang
Is heard and understood:
"Before the nations God as king
Reigns from his throne of wood."

This wood, now spread with purple, wears
The pageantry of kings;
Of chosen stock it dares to hold
On high his tortured limbs.

O blessed Tree, upon whose arms
The world's own ransom hung,
His body pays our debt, and life
From Satan's grasp is wrung.

O sacred Cross, our steadfast hope
In this our Passiontide,
Through you the Son obtained for all
Forgiveness as he died.

May every living creature praise
Our God both one and three,
Who rules in everlasting peace
All whom his cross makes free.

-Venantius Fortunatus

The *Vexilla regis prodeunt*, written by Venantius Fortunatus as a processional hymn to welcome a relic of the true Cross, has been the Church's traditional hymn during Passiontide until Holy Thursday. This translation is by Fr. Ralph Wright, O.S.B.

Man of Sorrows, Wrapt in Grief

Man of Sorrows, wrapt in grief,
Bow Thine ear to our relief;
Thou for us the path hast trod
Of the dreadful wrath of God;
Thou the cup of fire hast drained
Till its light alone remained.
Lamb of Love! we look to Thee:
Hear our mournful litany.

By the garden, fraught with woe,
Whither Thou full oft wouldst go;
By Thine agony of prayer
In the desolation there;
By the dire and deep distress
Of that myst'ry fathomless:
Lord, our tears in mercy see:
Hearken to our litany.

By the chalice brimming o'er
With disgrace and torment sore;
By those lips which fain would pray
That it might but pass away;
By the heart which drank it dry,
Lest a rebel race should die;
Be Thy pity, Lord, our plea:
Hear our solemn litany.

Man of Sorrows! let Thy grief
Purchase for us our relief;
Lord of mercy! bow Thine ear,
Slow to anger, swift to hear;
By the Cross's royal road
Lead us to the throne of God,
There for aye to sing to Thee
Heav'n's triumphant litany.

-Matthew Bridges

Matthew Bridges (1800–1894), the author of many hymns, is the translator of this work from a Slovak hymnal. It was set to music by Nicola Montani (1880–1948), the American church-music composer, scholar, and director, and one of the founders of the Society of St. Gregory of America.

All Glory, Laud, and Honor

All, glory, laud, and honor
To Thee, Redeemer King,
To whom the lips of children
Made sweet hosannas ring.
Thou art the King of Israel
Thou David's royal Son,
Who in the Lord's name comest
The King and blessed One.

The company of angels
Are praising Thee on high,
And mortal men and all things
Created make reply.
The people of the Hebrews
With palms before Thee went;
Our praise and pray'r and anthems
Before Thee we present.

To Thee before Thy passion
They sang their hymns of praise;
To Thee now high exalted
Our melody we raise.
Thou didst accept their praises,
Accept the pray'rs we bring,
Who in all good delightest,
Thou good and gracious King.

-Theodulph of Orleans

This early ninth-century work (*Gloria, laus et honor*) is attributed to
Theodulph of Orleans, the Visigoth scholar at Charlemagne's court,
and has been sung for centuries as the processional hymn on Palm
Sunday. This familiar rendering is by John Mason Neale (1818–66),
a high-church Anglican clergyman and one of the most prolific and
masterful hymn translators of the nineteenth century.

Ye Sons and Daughters of the Lord

Alleluia, Alleluia, Alleluia! (refrain)

Ye sons and daughters of the Lord!
The King of glory, the King adored,
This day Himself from death restored.
Alleluia!
(Refrain)

All in the early morning grey
Went holy women on their way,
To see the tomb where Jesus lay.
Alleluia!
(Refrain)

Of spices pure a precious store
In their pure hands those women bore,
To anoint the Sacred Body o'er.
Alleluia!
(Refrain)

Then straightway One in white they see,
Who saith, "Ye seek the Lord; but He
Is ris'n, and gone to Galilee."
Alleluia!
(Refrain)

This told they Peter, told they John,
Who forthwith to the tomb are gone;
But Peter is by John outrun.
Alleluia!
(Refrain)

That selfsame night, while out of fear
The doors were shut, their Lord most dear
To His apostles did appear.

Alleluia!
(Refrain)

But Thomas when of this he heard,
Was doubtful of his brethren's word;
Wherefore again there comes the Lord.
Alleluia!
(Refrain)

"Thomas, behold my Side," saith He;
"My Hands, my Feet, my Body see,
And doubt not, but believe in Me."
Alleluia!
(Refrain)

When Thomas saw that wounded Side,
The truth no longer he denied;
"Thou art my Lord and God," he cried.
Alleluia!
(Refrain)

Oh, blest are they who have not seen
Their Lord, and yet believe in Him;
Eternal life awaiteth them.
Alleluia!
(Refrain)

Now let us praise the Lord most high,
And strive His Name to magnify
On this great day through earth and sky.
Alleluia!
(Refrain)

Whose mercy ever runneth o'er,
Whom men and angel hosts adore,
To Him be glory ever more.
Alleluia!
(Refrain)

-Edward Caswall

This twelve-stanza Latin hymn may have been written as early as the thirteenth or as late as the seventeenth century. In many French churches it is a traditional part of Benediction of the Blessed Sacrament after Easter Vespers. This translation of *O filii et filiae* is by Fr. Edward Caswall, who, along with John Mason Neale, was the most influential translator of Latin hymns.

Victimae Paschali Laudes

Forth to the paschal Victim, Christians, bring
Your sacrifice of praise;

The Lamb redeems the sheep;
And Christ, the sinless One,
Hath to the Father sinners reconciled.

Together, death and life
In a strange conflict strove.
The Prince of life, who died,
Now lives and reigns.

What thou sawest, Mary, say,
As thou wentest on the way.

I saw the tomb wherein the living one had lain.
I saw His glory as He rose again;
Napkin and linen clothes, and angels twain:
Yea, Christ is risen, my hope, and He
Will go before you into Galilee.

We know that Christ indeed has risen from the grave:
Hail, thou King of Victory,
Have mercy, Lord, and save.
Amen. Alleluia.

-Author Unknown

The Sequence of the Easter Sunday Mass (and, formerly, repeated during the Easter octave) is a work in six (originally seven) strophes of masterfully rhythmical Latin. Its authorship, long contested, has been attributed to Wipo, chaplain to the eleventh-century Holy Roman Emperor Conrad II.